300 AIR FRYER RECIPES

DELICIOUS EASY METHOD COOKBOOK

JUSTIN RAMSEY

WHY YOU SHOULD READ THIS BOOK

If you are the excited owner of a new Air Fryer, this book will help to provide some inspiration and meal ideas.
New users may struggle to do more than reheat leftovers with this great machine and I felt that there should be a comprehensive resource out there. I have tried and tested a whopping 300 recipes from a range of genres for your perusal. My family regularly enjoy using this appliance and I hope yours will too!

Justin

TABLE OF CONTENTS

INTRODUCTION 15

BREAKFAST 17

APPLE OAT FRITTERS 17

BAKED EGGS 18

BAKED EGGS WITH SAUSAGE AND TOASTIES 19

SAUSAGE AND TOMATO FRITTATA 20

BREAKFAST SANDWICH 21

CHEESY BACON CROQUETTES 22

CORN FRITTERS 23

CREAMY SCRAMBLED EGGS WITH TOMATOES AND SPINACH 24

CRISPY BACON 25

FRENCH TOAST SOLDIERS 26

MUSHROOM AND FETA FRITTATA 27

OATMEAL MUFFINS 28

POTATO ROSTI 29

RAREBIT WITH FRIED EGG 30

SCRAMBLED EGGS 31

THAI STYLE OMELETTE 32

SIDES 33

BACON AND GARLIC SPINACH 33

BACON PAPRIKA POTATOES 34

BAKED POTATOES 35

BAKED ZUCCHINI FRIES 36

BROCCOLI TOTS 37

CAULIFLOWER BITES 38

CAULIFLOWER FRIED RICE 39

CAULIFLOWER MELTS 40

CHEESY BROCCOLI ROUNDS 41

CHEESY GARLIC BREAD 42

CHEESY POLENTA 43

CORN CUTLET 44

CORNBREAD LOAF 45

CRISPY BEANS 46

CRISPY BROCOLLI 47

CRISPY CARROTS 48

CRISPY POTATO WEDGES 49

CRISPY TATER TOTS 50

CURRIED VEGETABLE SAMOSA 51

FETA WEDGES 52

FRENCH FRIES 53

FRIED GREEN TOMATOES 54

FRIED TOFU 55

FRITTO MISTO 56

GARLIC AND WHITE WINE MUSHROOMS 57

GARLIC SQUASH 58

GARLIC STUFFED MUSHROOMS 59

GREEN BEANS WITH PARSLEY ALMONDS 60

GRILLED TOMATOES 61

HEIRLOOM TOMATOES WITH FETA 62

HOMEMADE CROUTONS 63

JAPANESE ASPARAGUS FRIES 64

LEMON GREEN BEANS 65

LEMON HERB ROASTED POTATOES 66

MAPLE ROASTED PARSNIPS 67

MUSHROOM KIDNEY BEAN QUINOA 68

ONION RINGS 69

PARMESAN ZUCCHINI CHIPS 70

PLANTAIN FRITTERS 71

POTATO GRATIN 72

POTATO STUFFED BREAD 73

ROAST PUMPKIN WITH STUFFING 74

ROAST WINTER VEGETABLES 75

ROASTED BRUSSEL SPROUTS 76

ROASTED EGGPLANT 77

SEEDED BROWN LOAF 78

SHRIMP FRIED RICE 79

SMASHED FINGERLING POTATOES 80

SPICY PARSNIP CHIPS 81

STUFFED MUSHROOMS WITH SOUR CREAM 82

STUFFED PEPPERS 83

STUFFED PORTOBELLO MUSHROOMS 84

SWEET POTATO FRIES 85

SNACKS 86

ASIAN ROASTED CHICKEN WINGS 86

BACON WRAPPED SHRIMP 87

BAJA FISH TACOS 88

BANANA CHIPS 89

BASIL RICOTTA BALLS 90

BEEF AND FETA RICE BALLS 91

BEEF AND VEGETABLE MEATBALLS 92

BEEF CHILI 93

BLACK-EYED PEA AND HAM BITES 94

BLOOMING ONION 95

BUFFALO CHICKEN EGG ROLLS 96

BUTTERFLIED SHRIMP 97

BUTTERMILK CHICKEN 98

CAJIN SHRIMP 99

CARAMELIZED CHESTNUTS 100

CATFISH NUGGETS 101

CELERY PRAWNS 102

CHEESE AND BACON BREAD BAKE 103

CHEESE CORN AND SPINACH SQUARES 104

CHEESE CRACKERS 106

CHEESE MOCHI BALLS 107

CHEESE-STEAK EGG ROLLS 108

CHICKEN AND CREAM CHEESE PASTRIES 109

CHICKEN NUGGETS 110

CHILEAN FRIED CALZONES 111

CHILI CHICKPEA BITES 112

CHILI TUNA PUFFS 113

CHINESE WONTONS 114

CHORIZO EMPANADES 115

CLAM FRITTERS 116

CORN DOGS 117

CORN TORTILLA CHIPS 118

CRAB AND FENNEL WONTONS 119

CRAB CAKES   120

CRAB CROQUETTES   121

CRANBERRY MEATBALLS   123

CREPE WRAPPED PRAWNS   124

CRISP SPICY TUNA SUSHI   125

CRISPY BOCCONCINI   126

CRISPY CHICKEN WONTONS   127

CRISPY HOT PRAWNS WITH COCKTAIL SAUCE   128

CRUMBED CHICKEN STRIPS   129

DUTCH CROQUETTES   130

FALAFEL WITH CUCUMBER SAUCE   131

FETA TRIANGLES   133

FILIPINO FRIED CHICKEN   134

FISH SANDWICHES   135

FLAVOURSOME MEATBALLS   136

FRIED BEEF ROLLS   137

FRIED CALAMARI   138

FRIED CRAB STICKS   139

FRIED GREEN SPANISH OLIVES   140

FRIED GRILLED CHEESE SANDWICH BITES   141

FRIED OYSTERS   142

FRIED PEANUT BUTTER AND JELLY SANDWICHES   143

FRIED PICKLES   144

FRIED RAVIOLI   145

HERB AND GARLIC FISH FINGERS   146

HOMEMADE NACHOS   147

INDIAN NAVAJO FRY BREAD   148

JALAPENO BITES 149

JERK CHICKEN WINGS 150

KALE CHIPS 151

LASAGNA CUPCAKES 152

LEMON FRIED CHORIZO 153

LEMONED TUNA PATTIES 154

MACARONI AND CHEESE ROUNDS 155

MEATBALLS IN TOMATO SAUCE 156

MEDITERRANEAN CHICKEN BITES 157

MOROCCAN MEATBALLS WITH MINT DIP 158

MOZZARELLA CHEESE STICKS 159

NACHO PRAWNS 160

POT STICKERS 161

POTATO AND ARUGULA CROQUETTES 162

POTATO CROQUETTES 163

PORK FRIES 164

PRAWN AND PORK NOODLE BALLS 165

PROSCUITTO AND SPINACH ARANCINI 166

REUBEN EGG ROLLS 167

RISOTTO BALLS 168

ROSEMARY RUSSET POTATO CHIPS 169

SALMON CROQUETTES 170

SALT AND PEPPER CHICKEN WINGS 171

SAUERKRAUT BALLS 172

SAUSAGE AND SAGE STUFFING BALLS 173

SAUSAGE ROLLS 174

SEAFOOD SKEWERS WITH LIME MAYONNAISE 175

SESAME PRAWN TOASTS 176

SLOPPY JOE'S 177

SOFT SHELL CRAB 178

SOUTHERN STYLE FRIED CHICKEN 179

SPICY BARBEQUE DRUMSTICKS 180

SPICY CHEESE BALLS 181

SPRING ROLLS 182

TAIWANESE POPCORN CHICKEN 183

TUNA BITES 184

VEGETABLE CHIPS 185

VEGETABLE SPRING ROLLS 186

ZUCCHINI PATTIES 187

MAIN MEALS 188

BALSAMIC GARLIC CHICKEN BREAST 188

BBQ PORK FOR SANDWICHES 189

BEEF BURGERS 190

BEEF SCHNITZEL 191

BEEF STROGANOFF 192

BEEF WITH BEANS 193

BLACK BEAN VEGGIE BURGERS 194

BOLOGNAISE SAUCE 195

BREADED SPAM STEAKS 196

CAJUN CORN MEAL BREADED CHICKEN 197

CARAMEL APPLE PORK CHOPS 198

CHAR SIEW PORK 199

CHEESY PAPRIKA CHICKEN 200

CHEESY TURKEY MEATLOAF 201

CHICKEN LIME TAQUITOS	202
CHICKEN TIKKA	203
CHIMICHURRI STEAK	204
CHINESE BRAISED PORK BELLY	205
CHINESE PORK RIBS	206
CHIPOTLE CHICKEN	207
COCONUT CORIANDER TILAPIA	208
COCONUT SHRIMP	209
COCONUT TUMERIC CHICKEN	210
CRISPY ROAST PORK	211
CRUMBED FISH	212
DIJONAISE SALMON	213
FINGER STEAKS	214
FISH AND CHIPS	215
FRIED CHICKEN CUTLET	216
FRIED QUAIL WITH SPICY SALT	217
GARLIC LAMB CHOPS	218
GARLIC MARINATED STEAK	219
GINGER BEEF	220
GINGER GLAZED MAHI MAHI	221
GREEK KEFTEDE MEATBALLS	222
GRILLED SALMON	223
HONEY GLAZED SALMON	224
HONEY MUSTARD CHICKEN	225
HONEY SESAME PRAWNS	226
ITALIAN BREADED PORK CHOPS	227
ITALIAN SAUSAGE AND PEPPERS	228

ITALIAN STYLE FISH   229

KEY WEST CHICKEN   230

KOREAN STYLE CHICKEN TENDERS   231

LAMB KIBBEH   232

LEMON ROSEMARY CHICKEN   233

LEMONGRASS BEEF   234

MARINATED LAMB CHOPS   235

MEAT LOAF   236

MEXICAN CHICKEN KABOBS   237

MEXICAN FRIED FISH   238

MOCHIKO CHICKEN   239

MUSHROOM AND PEPPERONI PIZZA   240

MUSHROOM TARRAGON CHICKEN   241

MUSTARD CHICKEN   242

OAT CRUSTED FISH   243

ORANGE CHICKEN AND BROWN RICE   244

PARMESAN BREADED PORK CHOPS   245

PARMIGIANA SCHNITZEL   246

PEANUT SATAY PORK   247

PORK CUTLET ROLLS   248

PORK TENDERS WITH BELL PEPPERS   249

POTATO CRUSTED BEEF TENDERS   250

PRAWN PASTED CHICKEN   251

RATATOUILLE   252

ROASTED CORNISH GAME HEN   253

ROASTED MACADAMIA LAMB   254

SALMON PATTIES   255

SALMON QUICHE	256
SALMON RISSOLES	257
SALMON WITH DILL SAUCE	258
SNAPPER WITH ASIAN DRESSING	259
SOBA SALMON NOODLES	261
SPICY BEEF	262
SPINACH AND FETA PIE	263
SPINACH QUICHE	265
SPINACH STUFFED CHICKEN BREAST	266
STICKY BARBEQUE PORK RIBS	267
SWEET AND SOUR CHICKEN	268
TANDOORI CHICKEN	269
TERIYAKI CHICKEN	270
THAI BASIL CHICKEN	271
THAI FISH CAKES WITH MANGO RELISH	272
THAI FRIED CHICKEN	273
TOMATO AND CHICKEN PASTA	274
TURKEY AND MUSHROOM PATTIES	275
TURKEY CHEESEBURGER MEATLOAF	276
TURKEY QUINOA MEATLOAF	277
VEAL KEBAB	278
VEAL SAFFRON RISOTTO	279
VENISON BACKSTRAP	280
ZUCCHINI AND PEPPER RISOTTO	281
DESSERTS AND SWEETS	282
APPLE PASTRY DUMPLINGS	282
BERRY PANCAKE TOPPING	283

BAKED ALASKAS	284
BANANA AND RHUBARB SLICE	285
BANANA CAKE	286
BANANAS IN COCONUT BATTER	287
BLUEBERRY MUFFINS	288
BUTTER CAKE	289
BUTTER COOKIES	290
CHERRY CLAFOUTIS	291
CHOCOLATE BROWNIES	292
CHOCOLATE CAKE	293
CHOCOLATE CHERRY POUND CAKE	294
CHOCOLATE FONDANT	295
CINNAMON CRISPAS	296
CINNAMON DOUGHNUTS	297
COCONUT FLAN	298
CRUNCHY SNICKERS	299
FRIED BANANAS	300
FRIED CHOC CHIP COOKIE DOUGH	301
FRIED MADERIA ICE CREAM BITES	302
FRIED MARS BARS	303
FRIED OREOS	304
FRIED STRAWBERRIES	305
FRUIT CAKE	306
FRUIT MUFFINS	307
GLAZED HONEY PEARS	308
LEMON CREAM CHEESE BARS	309
LEMON MERINGUE SPONGE	310

LEMON MUFFINS 311

MARBLE CAKE 312

MATCHA ALMOND COOKIES 313

MINI APPLE PIES 314

PANDAN CHIFFON CAKE 315

PEANUT COOKIES 317

RED VELVET CUPCAKES 318

SPICY PINEAPPLE FRITTERS 319

SUGARED BEIGNETS 320

TWICE BAKED NUT COOKIES 321

VANILLA SOUFFLE 322

About The Author 323

One Last Thing... 324

INTRODUCTION

What is an Air Fryer?
The Air Fryer is an appliance which offers a healthy alternative to deep frying food. Rather than submerging the food into oil and hot fat, the machine uses rapid hot air to circulate around and cook meals. This enables the outside of your food to be crispy, whilst ensuring that the inside layers are cooked through.

Benefits of an Air Fryer
- Healthier, oil-free meals
- Elimination of cooking odors through internal air filters
- Easier to clean due to lack of oil grease
- Versatility as Air Fryers are able to bake, grill, roast and fry
- Safer method of cooking compared to deep frying with exposed hot oil
- Ability to set and leave as most models include a digital timer
- Able to multitask cooking different ingredients using a separator

Guide to using this Recipe Book
There are numerous models of Air Fryers on the market, each with differing functions and operations. This book aims to act as a guide for all Air Fryer owners and requires a degree of flexibility in interpreting the recipe instructions.

Note that many of these recipes require additional baking utensils or trays/ramekins which fit inside of your Air Fryer, this is highlighted using asterisks in the recipes. It is difficult to cater across the broad range of appliances on the market as some have trays which hold liquid and some use a basket. Please use commonsense when cooking (if something is runny then place appropriate oven safe tray inside the Air Fryer).

This ensures that you get the benefit of crispy food without the necessity of hot oil.

If your Air Fryer uses a preset temperature then disregard the temperature setting for each recipe.

If your Air Fryer does not automatically stir the ingredients then you should do this manually to ensure even cooking. Use a plastic or wooden utensil to minimize any damage to your machine.

All recipes detail temperature settings in Fahrenheit (°F).

BREAKFAST

APPLE OAT FRITTERS

Ingredients
2 Apples, peeled, cored and sliced into rings
1/2 Cup Plus 2 Tbsps Sugar
1 ½ Tsps Ground Cinnamon
1/2 Cup Rice Flour
2 Tbsps Cornstarch
1 Tsp Baking Powder
3/4 Tsp Kosher Salt
1/2 Cup Club Soda
1 Cup Oats
1 Egg

Directions
1. Whisk 1/2 cup sugar and 1 teaspoon of cinnamon in a shallow bowl
2. Preheat the Air Fryer to 350 degrees
3. Pulse the oats in a food processor to a coarse powder. Transfer to a large bowl and whisk in rice flour, cornstarch, baking powder, salt, and remaining sugar and cinnamon. Whisk in egg and club soda, adding more soda gradually until the mixture forms the consistency of pancake batter
4. Dip apple rings into the batter and place into the Air Fryer tray in batches. Cook for 4 minutes until golden brown and crisp
5. Transfer fritters onto a plate then sprinkle with reserved cinnamon sugar

BAKED EGGS

Ingredients
4 Eggs
Butter
1 Tbsp Olive Oil
1 lb Baby Spinach
7 Ozs Leg Ham
4 Tsps Full Cream Milk
Salt and Pepper to taste
* 4 x Oven Safe Ramekins

Directions
1. Preheat the Air Fryer to 350 degrees
2. Smear a layer of butter into each ramekin
3. Divide out the spinach and ham equally over the four ramekins
4. Crack an egg into each and add 1 teaspoon of milk
5. Season with salt and pepper
6. Place into Air Fryer for about 15 (runny yolk) to 20 minutes (fully cooked) until the egg sets

BAKED EGGS WITH SAUSAGE AND TOASTIES

Ingredients
3 Eggs
1/4 Cup Milk
2 Sausages, cooked and sliced
1 Slice Bread, cut into sticks
1/4 Cup Grated Cheese
Cooking Spray
* 3 x Oven Safe Ramekins

Directions
1. Preheat the Air Fryer to 350 degrees
2. Whisk together the eggs and milk until fluffy
3. Spray ramekins with cooking oil then divide the egg mixture between them
4. Add slices of sausage, then place four small bread pieces around the edges, pushing them down to absorb some of the egg mixture. Top with a little grated cheese
5. Place the three ramekins inside the Air Fryer and set the dial to 20 minutes. You can check after 10 minutes to see how they are going
6. Serve as is or with extra salad on the side

SAUSAGE AND TOMATO FRITTATA

Ingredients
3 Eggs
1/2 Breakfast Sausage
5 Grape Tomatoes
1/2 Tbsp Olive Oil
1/4 Cup Chopped Parsley
1/4 Cup Parmesan Cheese
Salt and Pepper to taste
* Round Baking Tray

Directions
1. Preheat the Air Fryer to 350 degrees
2. Slice the tomatoes in half and place with the sausage in the Air Fryer for 6 minutes
3. Add the oil, eggs, parsley, cheese and salt and pepper into a bowl and combine well
4. Open the Air Fryer tray and pour the mixture over the tomatoes and sausage. Allow to cook for a further 6 minutes to until eggs are done to desired wellness

BREAKFAST SANDWICH

Ingredients
1 Egg
1 English Muffin
2 Bacon Slices
Salt and Pepper to taste
* Oven Safe Soufflé Cup

Directions
1. Crack the egg into the soufflé cup and season with salt and pepper
2. Heat the Air Fryer to 390 degrees and place the soufflé cup, bacon and English muffin into the tray
3. Cook all ingredients for 6 minutes or longer depending on preference
4. Assemble sandwich and enjoy

CHEESY BACON CROQUETTES

Ingredients
For the Filling:
1 lb Cheddar Cheese
1 lb Bacon Slices

For the Coating:
1 ½ Tbsps Olive Oil
1 Cup Flour
2 Eggs, whisked
1/2 Cup Panko Breadcrumbs

Directions
1. Cut the cheddar cheese into 5 portions
2. Take two bacon slices and wrap them around each cheddar portion, covering completely
3. Place the pieces into the freezer for 10 minutes to harden but be careful not to freeze
4. Set the Air Fryer to 350 degrees
5. Mix together the panko and oil, stirring well. Place each semi frozen croquette into the flour to coat. Then place into the eggs and the panko oil mixture
6. Place the croquettes into the Air Fryer and cook for 8 minutes or until crispy
7. Serve with tomato or spicy sauce

CORN FRITTERS

Ingredients
1 Cup Corn Kernels
1 Cup Flour
1½ Tsps Baking Powder
1/2 Tsp Salt
1/4 Tsp Pepper
3/4 Cup Milk
2 Tbsps Butter, melted
1 Egg

Directions
1. Preheat Air Fryer to 375 degrees
2. Mix the baking powder, flour, salt and pepper together in a bowl. In a separate bowl, whisk egg, milk, and butter together and stir into dry ingredients. Fold in the corn and allow batter to sit for 5 minutes
3. Take spoonfuls of the batter and form into small rounded fritters. Continue until all batter is used up. Then place fritters on a tray and freeze for 5 minutes to retain the shape
4. Place the fritters into the Air Fryer tray and cook for about 4 minutes
5. Serve with yoghurt or salsa dip

CREAMY SCRAMBLED EGGS WITH TOMATOES AND SPINACH

Ingredients
1/4 Cup Baby Spinach
15 Cherry Tomatoes
2 Tsps Olive Oil
1 Cup Cream
Sea Salt
4 Eggs
* Round Baking Tray

Directions
1. Break the eggs into a large bowl then add the cream and sea salt to taste
2. Preheat the Air Fryer at 300 degrees. Drop the oil in the baking tray and tilt pan to spread evenly
3. Place the baking tray filled with the egg and cream mixture into the Air Fryer for 8 min
4. Cut the tomatoes into small pieces and mix with spinach. Add to the Air Fryer for another minute
5. Open every few minutes to whisk continuously until it becomes fluffy and yellow
6. Remove ingredients and serve

CRISPY BACON

Ingredients
1 lb Sliced Bacon
3 Cups All Purpose Flour
Salt and Pepper to taste
1/2 Cup Milk
3 Eggs

Directions
1. Whisk together the eggs and milk in a bowl until smooth. Separate the bacon strips, and soak in the milk mixture for 30 minutes
2. Preheat the Air Fryer to 340 degrees
3. Whisk together the flour, salt, and pepper in a separate bowl. Remove the bacon from the egg mixture, and toss with the flour to coat
4. Place bacon into the Air Fryer tray and fry for about 4 minutes until golden brown or more for desired crispness

FRENCH TOAST SOLDIERS

Ingredients
4 Slices of Bread
2 Tbsps Butter
2 Eggs
1/2 Tsp Cinnamon
Pinch of Salt
Pinch of Nutmeg
Pinch of Ground Cloves
Cooking Spray
Icing Sugar and Maple Syrup to serve

Directions
1. Preheat the Air Fryer to 350 degrees
2. In a bowl, gently beat together the eggs, salt, nutmeg, cloves, and cinnamon
3. Butter both sides of each bread slice and cut into strips
4. Soak each bread strip in the egg mixture and arrange in the Air Fryer tray. You may have to cook these in two batches
5. Cook for 2 minutes and take out the strips to lightly coat the bread with cooking spray on both sides
6. Return tray to the Air Fryer and cook for 4 more minutes, checking after a couple minutes to ensure they are cooking evenly
7. When the bread is golden brown, remove from Air Fryer
8. To garnish and serve, sprinkle soldiers with icing sugar and drizzle with maple syrup

MUSHROOM AND FETA FRITTATA

Ingredients
2 Cups Button Mushrooms, sliced
3 Tbsps Feta Cheese, crumbled
1/2 Red Onion, sliced
1 Tbsp Olive Oil
1 Pinch Salt
Cooking Spray
3 Eggs
* Round Baking Tray

Directions
1. In a sauté pan with olive oil, cook the onions and mushrooms under a medium flame until tender
2. Preheat the Air Fryer to 340 degrees
3. In a mixing bowl, crack the eggs and whisk thoroughly, adding a pinch of salt
4. Coat the baking tray with the cooking spray. Pour the eggs into the tray, then the onion and mushroom mixture and then the cheese
5. Place the tray in the Air Fryer and cook for 10 to 12 minutes. The frittata is done when you can stick a knife into the middle, and the knife comes out clean

OATMEAL MUFFINS

Ingredients
3 ½ Ozs Oats
3 Ozs Butter, melted
1/2 Cup Icing Sugar
1/2 Cup Flour
1/4 Tsp Vanilla Essence
Pinch of Baking Powder
1 Tbsp Raisins
Cooking Spray
2 Eggs
* Silicon Muffin Molds

Directions
1. Mix together the sugar and butter until it forms a soft consistency
2. Beat the eggs together with the vanilla essence and add to the sugar and butter mix until soft peaks form
3. In a separate bowl, mix in the oats, raisins, flour and baking powder. Combine contents with the remaining mixed ingredients
4. Lightly grease the muffin molds with cooking spray. Fill each mold with the batter mixture
5. Preheat the Air Fryer at 350 degrees
6. Place muffin molds into the Air Fryer tray and cook for 12 minutes
7. Allow to cool before serving

POTATO ROSTI

Ingredients
5 lbs Potatoes
1/4 Cup Olive Oil
2 Onions, grated
1 Tbsp Salt
3/4 Teaspoon Pepper
2 Cups Grated Swiss Cheese

Directions
1. Preheat the Air Fryer at 350 degrees
2. Place onions in a large bowl. Peel potatoes and then grate into the largest holes of a box grater, adding them to the bowl. Squeeze handfuls of the mixture to release excess liquid
3. Add salt, pepper, cheese, and oil to the potato mixture and toss well to combine
4. Taking balls of the mixture, compress into thin patties
5. Bake rosti patties until golden in the Air Fryer for approximately 15 minutes
6. Serve with relish or topped with egg

RAREBIT WITH FRIED EGG

Ingredients
1 ½ Cups Grated Mature Cheddar
1/3 Cup Ale
1 Tsp Mustard Powder
1/2 Tsp Paprika
2 Tsps Worcestershire Sauce
4 Slices Sourdough
4 Fried Eggs
Black Pepper to taste

Directions
1. Place the eggs in a pan sunny side up and fry until desired doneness is achieved. Set aside
2. Preheat the Air Fryer to 350 degrees
3. Combine the cheddar with mustard powder, paprika, Ale and Worcestershire sauce
4. Spread one side of each sourdough slice with the cheddar mixture. Then place bread slices into the Air Fryer tray and cook until slightly browned for about 3 minutes
5. Top each rarebit with a fried egg and season to taste with pepper

SCRAMBLED EGGS

Ingredients
2 Eggs
2 Tsps Melted Butter
Salt and Pepper to taste
* Round Baking Tray

Directions
1. Break the 2 eggs and whisk until fluffy
2. Preheat Air Fryer at 280 degrees
3. Drop the butter in the baking tray to grease evenly
4. Pour the beaten egg into the tray and place in the Air Fryer for 8 minutes. If you would like other ingredients in your eggs such as mushrooms, tomatoes, or cheese, drop them in at this point
5. Open every few minutes to whisk continuously until it becomes fluffy and yellow

THAI STYLE OMELETTE

Ingredients
2 Eggs
3 ½ Ozs Minced Pork
1 Cup Onion
1 Tbsp Fish Salt

Directions
1. Chop the onion and set aside
2. Beat the eggs until light and fluffy
3. Preheat the Air Fryer to 280 degrees
4. Combine all ingredients in a bowl
5. Pour the mixture into the Air Fryer tray
6. Set timer for 10 minutes or until the mixture turns golden brown
7. Cut into portions and serve

SIDES

BACON AND GARLIC SPINACH

Ingredients
1 Onion, sliced thinly
1 Garlic Clove, minced
3 Slices Bacon Rasher
2 Tsps Olive Oil
4 Ozs Spinach

Directions
1. Preheat Air Fryer to 340 degrees
2. Heat oil for 2 minutes in the Air Fryer. Add onion, garlic and bacon into tray and cook for 3 minutes
3. Once the mixture is crispy, add spinach to the tray and cook for another 4 minutes or until the leaves have been sautéed

BACON PAPRIKA POTATOES

Ingredients
3 Potatoes
5 Rashers Smoked Bacon
1 Tsp Salt
1 Tbsp Olive Oil
2 Tsps Paprika

Directions
1. Peel the potatoes and cut into even cubes
2. Coat cubes with olive oil and season with salt
3. Heat the Air Fryer to 360 degrees and cook the potatoes for 11 minutes or until golden brown
4. Dice the bacon and add into the Air Fryer. Cook for 3 additional minutes
5. Season with paprika to desired taste

BAKED POTATOES

Ingredients
4 Potatoes
Olive Oil

Directions
1. Peel the potatoes then them cut in half
2. Preheat the Air Fryer to 350 degrees
3. Brush the potatoes gently with the oil then cook them in the Air Fryer for 10 minutes
4. Brush again with the oil then continue to cook for another 10 minutes. Repeat the process once more if necessary as cooking time varies depending on potato size
5. Once they are cooked through, garnish with toppings of choice and serve

BAKED ZUCCHINI FRIES

Ingredients
3 Medium Zucchinis
2 Egg Whites
1/2 Cup Seasoned Breadcrumbs
2 Tbsp Grated Parmesan Cheese
1/4 Tsp Garlic Powder
Salt and Pepper to taste
Cooking spray

Directions
1. Slice the zucchinis lengthwise into sticks
2. In a bowl, beat egg whites and season with salt and pepper
3. In another bowl, mix breadcrumbs, garlic powder and cheese together
4. Dip the zucchini sticks into the egg and then into the bread crumb and cheese mixture
5. Place the breaded zucchini on a single layer in the Air Fryer tray and coat lightly with cooking spray on top
6. Bake at 390 degrees for about 15 minutes until golden brown
7. Serve with ranch or marinara sauce for dipping

BROCCOLI TOTS

Ingredients
2 Cups Broccoli Florets
1 ¼ Cup Panko Crumbs
1 ¼ Cup White Cheddar Cheese
1/4 Cup Parmesan Cheese
1 Tsp Kosher Salt
2 Eggs, beaten

Directions
1. Place dry broccoli florets in a bowl and blitz with a food processor until finely crumbed
2. In a large bowl, mix and combine broccoli, panko crumbs, both cheeses and salt. Add eggs and mix to combine
3. Roll spoonfuls of the mixture into small balls and place in the fridge for 30 minutes to hold the shape
4. Preheat the Air Fryer to 350 degrees
5. Place the broccoli tots into the Air Fryer and cook for 12 minutes until browned and crispy
6. Remove from tray and serve immediately

CAULIFLOWER BITES

Ingredients
1 Head Cauliflower, cut into small florets
2 Tsps Garlic Powder
Pinch of Salt and Pepper
1 Tbsp Butter, melted
1/2 Cup Chili Sauce
Olive Oil

Directions
1. Place cauliflower into a bowl and pour oil over florets to lightly cover
2. Season florets with salt, pepper and the garlic powder and toss well
3. Place florets into Air Fryer at 350 degrees for 14 minutes
4. Remove cauliflower from the Air Fryer. Combine the melted butter with the chili sauce
5. Pour over the florets so that they are well coated
6. Return to the Air Fryer and cook for additional 3 to 4 minutes
7. Serve as a side or with ranch or cheese dip as a snack

CAULIFLOWER FRIED RICE

Ingredients
1 Cauliflower
1 Tbsp Sesame Oil
1 Tbsp Peanut Oil
4 Tbsps Soy Sauce
4 Cloves Garlic, minced
1 Tbsp Grated Ginger
1/2 Cup Lemon Juice
8 Ozs Water Chestnuts, chopped
3/4 Cup Peas
2.2 lbs Canned Mushrooms
Coriander to garnish

Directions
1. Place the chestnuts, sesame oil, peanut oil, soy sauce, garlic, ginger and lemon juice into a bowl and mix well
2. Cut the cauliflower into small florets and whiz in a food processor until it is broken down to the size of rice grains. Combine with the bowl ingredients
3. Preheat the Air Fryer to 375 degrees
4. Place mixture into the Air Fryer and cook for 20 minutes
5. After 20 minutes, add the peas and the drained mushrooms and allow to cook for another 15 minutes
6. Serve hot garnished with coriander

CAULIFLOWER MELTS

Ingredients
Cauliflower Head, cut into 1/2-inch thick pieces
1/4 Cup Olive Oil
2 Garlic Cloves, minced
1 Tsp Salt
1/2 Tsp Black Pepper
1/4 Cup Shelled Pistachios
8 Slices Sourdough Bread
4 Ozs Comte Cheese Slices
2 Tbsps Chopped Parsley

Directions
1. Preheat the Air Fryer to 350 degrees
2. In a medium bowl, combine the oil, garlic, salt, and pepper. Add the cauliflower and toss to coat
3. Place the cauliflower into the Air Fryer and bake for 25 minutes until softened and crispy
4. In a saucepan over medium-high heat, toast the pistachios with a little oil. Allow to cool and then chop coarsely
5. Arrange the cauliflower on the bread slices. Sprinkle with pistachios and raisins and top with the cheese
6. Place topped slices into the Air Fryer until the cheese melts, 7 to 10 minutes
7. Top the toasts with chopped parsley and serve immediately

CHEESY BROCCOLI ROUNDS

Ingredients
16 Ozs Broccoli, chopped
3 Cups Shredded Cheddar Cheese
1 Cup Flour
1 Cup Breadcrumbs
Salt and Pepper to taste
3 Eggs

Directions
1. Whisk the eggs lightly and stir together with the broccoli and cheese and enough flour to make form a dough
2. Cover and refrigerate at least 2 hours
3. Compress the mixture into balls using spoonful's of the mix. Then roll each ball into the breadcrumbs to coat
4. Preheat the Air Fryer to 350 degrees
5. Fry the broccoli rounds in the Air Fryer tray in batches for 4 to 5 minutes. Ensure that they do not overlap
6. Serve with ranch dip

CHEESY GARLIC BREAD

Ingredients
2 Dinner Rolls
1/2 Cup Grated Parmesan Cheese
2 Tbsps Melted Butter
1 ½ Tbsps Garlic Powder
1 Tbsp Dried Parsley

Directions:
1. Cut the bread rolls top down into diagonal slices. Try to cut as far down as possible but not all the way through
2. Fill the slits with the grated cheese
3. Paint the tops of the rolls with the melted butter then sprinkle with the garlic powder and parsley
4. Place rolls into the Air Fryer at 350 degrees. Cook for 5 minutes or until the cheese is melted

CHEESY POLENTA

Ingredients
2 ½ Cups Cooked Polenta
1/4 Cup Parmesan, shaved
1 Cup Marinara Sauce
1 Tbsp Vegetable Oil
Salt to taste
*Baking Tray

Directions
1. Grease the baking tray with the oil
2. Place the polenta into the tray, ensuring that the top is evenly spread. Then place the tray into the fridge for 1 hour to firm
3. Preheat the Air Fryer to 350 degrees
4. Remove the tray from the fridge and cut the polenta into uniform slices
5. Place the polenta slices into the Air Fryer and cook for 5 to 6 minutes until crispy
6. Sprinkle with parmesan and season with salt
7. Serve with marinara on the side

CORN CUTLET

Ingredients
4 Potatoes
1 Cup Corn Kernels
1 Tbsp Vegetable Oil
1 Chopped Onion
3 Cloves Minced Garlic
1 Sprig Chopped Curry Leaves
3 Chopped Green Chilies
5 Stalks Chopped Coriander
Cooking Spray
1 Tsp Salt

For the Coating:
1 Beaten Egg
1 Cup Breadcrumbs

Directions
1. Boil the potatoes in a pot until soft to touch. Mash the potatoes and mix with boiled corn kernels
2. Add the oil, onions, garlic, curry leaves, green chilies, coriander and salt into the pot and mix together on low heat
3. Form mixture into small patties with even consistency
4. Dip each patty into the egg and then coat with the breadcrumbs
5. Preheat the Air Fryer to 390 degrees and cook each patty/cutlet for 12 minutes or until golden
6. Serve with chutney jam or salsa

CORNBREAD LOAF

Ingredients
1 ½ Cups Flour
1 ¼ Cups Cornmeal
3/4 Cup Sugar
1/2 Tsp Baking Powder
1/2 Tsp Baking Soda
1/2 Tsp Salt
2 Eggs
1/2 Cup Melted Margarine
1 Cup Buttermilk
1 Cup Corn Kernels
* Loaf Pan

Directions
1. Preheat the Air Fryer to 375 degrees
2. Coat the loaf pan with cooking spray and dust with corn meal
3. Mix the flour, cornmeal, sugar, baking powder, baking soda, and salt in a large bowl
4. Combine the eggs, melted margarine and milk in another bowl
5. Add the egg mixture and corn to dry ingredients and mix thoroughly. Pour the batter into the loaf pan
6. Place the pan into the Air Fryer and bake for 50 minutes to one hour until the loaf has risen
7. Slice and serve buttered whilst hot

CRISPY BEANS

Ingredients
9 Ozs Beans
1/2 Cup Flour
1/2 Tsps Garam Masala
1/2 Cup Breadcrumbs
2 Tsps Chili Powder
Salt to taste
2 Eggs
Olive Oil

Directions
1. Preheat the Air Fryer at 350 degrees
2. In a bowl, add flour, garam masala, chili powder, salt and mix well
3. Beat the eggs and set aside. On a separate plate, pour the breadcrumbs over
4. Take the beans and first coat them with the flour mixture, then dip into the egg mixture and then in the breadcrumbs. Repeat with all the remaining beans
5. Place the beans in the Air Fryer tray and cook for 4 minutes
6. Open the Air Fryer, coat the beans with little oil and again cook for 3 minutes to serve

CRISPY BROCOLLI

Ingredients
2 lbs Broccoli Florets
2 Tbsps Olive Oil
1 Tsp Kosher Salt
1/2 Tsp Black Pepper
2 Tsps Grated Lemon Zest
1/4 Cup Shaved Parmesan Cheese

Directions
1. Bring a saucepan filled with 6 cups of water to a boil over high heat. Once boiling, add the broccoli florets to the water and cook for 3 minutes. Remove from the water, drain well and toss with the olive oil, salt and pepper
2. Heat the Air Fryer to 390 degrees
3. Place the broccoli in the tray of the Air Fryer and cook for 12 minutes, tossing halfway through the cooking process to ensure even browning
4. Transfer cooked broccoli to a serving bowl. Toss with the lemon zest and parmesan cheese to serve

CRISPY CARROTS

Ingredients
4 Carrots
2 Tsps Sea Salt
1 Tbsp Olive Oil

Directions
1. Slice carrots lengthways ensuring they are of uniform thickness
2. Combine sea salt and olive oil in a bowl and drizzle over carrots so they are evenly coated
3. Heat the Air Fryer to 360 degrees
4. Cook carrots for 12 minutes until they are crispy and serve immediately

CRISPY POTATO WEDGES

Ingredients
4 Russet Potatoes
1 Cup Water
3 Tbsps Oil
1 Tsp Paprika
1/4 Tsp Black Pepper
1/4 Tsp Salt

Directions
1. Scrub the potatoes under running water to clean. Do not remove the peel
2. Boil potatoes in salted water for 40 minutes or until tender. Cool completely in the refrigerator
3. In a mixing bowl, combine oil, paprika, salt and black pepper. Cut the cooled potatoes into quarters and lightly toss in the mixture of oil and spices
4. Preheat the Air Fryer to 390 degrees. Add half of the potato wedges into the tray and place them skin side down, being careful not to overcrowd
5. Cook each batch for 13 to 15 minutes or until golden brown
6. Serve with sour cream and sweet chili sauce

CRISPY TATER TOTS

Ingredients
3 Potatoes
2 Tsps Oil
3 Tsps Onion, minced
Salt and pepper to taste

Directions
1. Chop up the potatoes into slices and place in a pot of salted water to boil
2. Once the potatoes are slightly more than al dente, remove from water
3. Mash the potatoes with the oil, onion, salt and pepper
4. Set your Air Fryer to 375 degrees. Form the potato mixture into tater tots about 3cm in length and bake for 8 minutes
5. Remove tray to toss and then bake for another 5 minutes until crispy

CURRIED VEGETABLE SAMOSA

Ingredients
3 Sheets Puff Pastry
2 Large Potatoes, peeled
1/2 Cup Onion, diced
2 Garlic Cloves, minced
2 Tbsps Ginger, grated
1/2 Cup Green Peas
1/2 Cup Carrot, diced
1 Tsp Garam Masala
1 Tbsp Curry Powder
Salt and Pepper to taste

Directions
1. Boil the potatoes in salted water and mash well once cooked through
1. In a saucepan, sauté the carrots, onion, ginger and garlic until tender and add to mashed potatoes
2. Add green peas and spices, then season with salt and pepper to personal taste
3. Cut the puff pastry sheets into quarters, then cut each quarter into a circular shape
4. Place two tablespoons of filling into each pastry circle and moisten edges with water. Fold the pastry in half and seal edges well using a fork
5. Preheat the Air Fryer to 390 degrees
6. Working in batches, fry samosas for 5 minutes each until golden brown and crispy

FETA WEDGES

Ingredients
1 Egg Yolk
5 Ozs Feta
2 Tbsps Parsley, chopped
5 Sheets Puff Pastry
Salt and Black Pepper to taste

Directions
1. Preheat the Air Fryer at 390 degrees
2. In a bowl, whisk the egg yolk, salt and pepper, feta, and parsley together
3. Cut each sheet of filo pastry into three even strips
4. Take a spoonful of the mixture and place in the center of each pastry strip. Fold the tip of each pastry to form a triangle and cross over until the filling is enclosed. You can use water to moisten and secure the edges together
5. Place the triangles into the Air Fryer and cook for 3 minutes until they are golden brown and crispy
6. Serve with sweet chili sauce

FRENCH FRIES

Ingredients
2 Russet Potatoes, washed and peeled
1 Tbsp Olive Oil

Directions:
1. Cut the potatoes into thin even strips. Cover the potatoes in water and soak for half an hour. Drain the strips well and ensure they are dry to the touch
2. Preheat the Air Fryer to 320 degrees
3. Place the fries into a bowl and toss to coat evenly with the olive oil
4. Place the potatoes into the Air Fryer and cook for 6 minutes. Remove fries from the tray and cool
5. Set the Air Fryer to 390 degrees and re-add the fries into the tray. Cook for a further 12 minutes or until crispy
6. Serve with ketchup or aioli

FRIED GREEN TOMATOES

Ingredients
4 Green Tomatoes, cut into 1/2 inch slices
2 Eggs
1/2 Cup Milk
1 Cup All Purpose Flour
1/2 Cup Cornmeal
1/2 Cup Breadcrumbs
2 Tsps Kosher Salt
1/4 Tsp Ground Black Pepper

Directions
1. Whisk the eggs and milk together in a bowl. Place the flour onto a shallow bowl. Combine the crumb, cornmeal and salt and pepper in a separate bowl
2. Coat the tomato slices in the flour to coat, then into the milk and then the egg mixture. Dredge in breadcrumbs to completely coat
3. Heat the Air Fryer to 340 degrees and place tomatoes on the tray in batches, ensuring that they do not overlap
4. Cook for about 6 minutes until they have browned on either side

FRIED TOFU

Ingredients
12 Ozs Firm Tofu
2 Tbsps Cornstarch
1/4 Cup Rice Flour
Salt and Pepper to taste
2 Tbsps Olive Oil

Directions
1. Preheat the Air Fryer to 350 degrees
2. Drain the tofu and cut into even cubes
3. In a separate bowl, mix together cornstarch and rice flour. Place the tofu pieces into the mixture and coat well
4. Drizzle oil onto tofu and transfer into the Air Fryer. Ensure that cubes are not overlapping
5. Cook cubes for 13 minutes. Shake the tray at the mid-point for even crispness
6. Season with salt and pepper. Serve with chili or soy sauce

FRITTO MISTO

Ingredients
9 Ozs Squid Tubes, sliced into rings
12 Green Prawns, peeled and deveined
14 Ozs White Fish, cut into 2cm pieces
3 ½ Ozs Whitebait
2 Zucchinis, thinly sliced
1 Bunch Asparagus
12 Sage Leaves
1 Cup Self Raising Flour
1 Tbsp Cornflour
1/2 Tsp Baking Soda
Sea Salt and Lemon Wedges to serve

Directions
1. Place seafood, vegetables and sage on paper towel to remove any excess moisture. Sift self raising flour and cornflour into a bowl, add baking soda and slowly whisk in 1 ½ cups of chilled water to form a smooth batter
2. Preheat the Air Fryer to 350 degrees
3. Work in batches to dip the vegetables, herbs and seafood into the batter and fry in the Air Fryer until golden, moving around to ensure that the pieces don't clump together
4. Remove, sprinkle with sea salt and serve with lemon wedges

GARLIC AND WHITE WINE MUSHROOMS

Ingredients
2 lbs Mushrooms
1 Tbsp Duck Fat
1/2 Tsp Garlic Powder
2 Tsps Herbes de Provence Mix
2 Tbsps White Vermouth

Directions
1. Preheat the Air Fryer to 350 degrees
2. Wash and dry the mushrooms. Cut each into quarters
3. Place the duck fat, garlic powder, and herbes de provence into the Air Fryer tray and heat for 2 minutes. Remove and stir with a wooden spoon if it clumps
4. Add the mushrooms to the tray and combine with mixture. Cook for 15 minutes
5. Once mushrooms have absorbed flavors and are tender to touch, add the white vermouth. Cook for another 5 minutes and serve

GARLIC SQUASH

Ingredients
1 Large Winter Squash
2 Tbsps Flour
8 Garlic Cloves, chopped
2 Tbsps Fresh Parsley, chopped
4 Tsps Olive Oil
Salt and Pepper to taste

Directions
1. Preheat the Air Fryer to 350 degrees
2. Wash and peel the squash, then cut into bite sized pieces
3. Coat the squash cubes with flour that has been seasoned lightly with salt and pepper
4. Put the squash into the Air Fryer, topping with garlic, olive oil and parsley. Shake to coat evenly
5. Bake for 30 minutes or just until squash is tender

GARLIC STUFFED MUSHROOMS

Ingredients
12 Mushrooms
1 Slice Bread
2 Garlic Cloves, minced
1 Tbsp Parsley
1 Tbsp Olive Oil
Black Pepper to season

Directions
1. Preheat the Air Fryer to 390 degrees
2. Grind the bread into fine crumbs using a food processor. Slowly add the oil, parsley, pepper and garlic
3. Remove the stalks from the mushrooms. Turn caps over and densely fill with the crumb mixture
4. Transfer the stuffed mushrooms into the Air Fryer and cook for 10 minutes or until they are lightly browned and crisp

GREEN BEANS WITH PARSLEY ALMONDS

Ingredients
8 Ozs Green Beans
1/2 Cup Slivered Almonds
1/2 Tbsp Olive Oil
1/4 Tsp Lemon Zest
1 Tbsp Lemon Juice
1/4 Cup Chopped Parsley
Salt and Pepper to taste

Directions
1. Wash and trim the green beans and cut them on an angle in halves
2. Place almonds into the Air Fryer and cook for 3 minutes at 350 degrees
3. Add the beans to the tray and drizzle with olive oil. Cook for an additional 7 minutes, until the beans are crisp but tender
4. Transfer the green beans and almonds to a serving bowl. Add the lemon zest, lemon juice, and parsley and stir to combine
5. Season with salt and pepper. Can be served warm or at room temperature in a salad

GRILLED TOMATOES

Ingredients
2 Tomatoes
1 Tsp Dried Mixed Herbs
Pepper to taste
Cooking Spray

Directions
1. Wash the tomatoes and cut into halves. Spray bottoms lightly with cooking spray
2. Sprinkle each halve with the mixed herbs and pepper
3. Place tomatoes into the Air Fryer tray cut-side up. Cook for 20 minutes at 320 degrees
4. Serve hot as a side dish

HEIRLOOM TOMATOES WITH FETA

Ingredients
For the Tomato:
1 Heirloom Tomato
8 Ozs Feta Cheese
1/2 Cup Red Onions, sliced paper thin
1 Tbsp Olive Oil
1 Pinch Salt

For the Basil Pesto:
1/2 Cup Parsley, chopped
1/2 Cup Basil, chopped
1/2 Cup Parmesan Cheese, grated
3 Tbsps Toasted Pine Nuts
1 Garlic Clove
1/2 Cup Olive Oil
1 Pinch Salt

Directions
1. To make the pesto, add parsley, basil, parmesan, garlic, toasted pine nuts and salt to a food processor. Turn on and slowly add the olive oil. Once all of the olive oil is incorporated into the pesto, store and refrigerate until ready to use
2. Preheat the Air Fryer to 350 degrees. Slice the tomato and the feta into half inch thick slices and pat tomato dry with a paper towel
3. Spread one tablespoon of the pesto on top of each tomato slice and top with the feta
4. Toss the red onions with the olive oil and place on top of the feta
5. Place the topped tomatoes into the Air Fryer tray and cook for 12 to 14 minutes or until the feta starts to soften and brown
6. Finish with a pinch of salt and an additional spoonful of basil pesto

HOMEMADE CROUTONS

Ingredients
5 Slices of Stale Bread
2 Tbsps Butter
1 Tbsp Olive Oil

Directions
1. Preheat the Air Fryer to 280 degrees
2. Cube the stale bread to desired size allowing for shrinkage as it cooks
3. Melt the butter and mix with the olive oil in a microwave or pan. Combine with the bread cubes until well coated
4. Place bread cubes into Air Fryer and cook for 3 minutes
5. Remove tray and toss cubes. Resume cooking for another 2 to 3 minutes
6. Cool completely and store in an airtight container

JAPANESE ASPARAGUS FRIES

Ingredients
8 Ozs Asparagus
1 Cup Cold Water
1 Egg, beaten
1 Cup Flour
1/8 Tsp Baking Soda
1/2 Cup Mayonnaise
2 Tbsps Chili Sauce
1 Green Onion, chopped

Directions
1. Wash and trim the woody ends of the asparagus spears. Mix the ice water and egg together in a bowl. Mix the flour and baking soda together in another bowl. Stir the flour mixture into the wet ingredients until combined
2. In a small bowl, mix the mayonnaise with the chili sauce to form a sauce
3. Preheat the Air Fryer to 350 degrees
4. Dip the asparagus spears in the batter to coat
5. Place the battered asparagus spears into the Air Fryer making sure they do not stick together. Fry until golden for 2 to 3 minutes
6. Serve the asparagus fries with the chili mayonnaise and topped with green onions for garnish

LEMON GREEN BEANS

Ingredients
1 lb Green Beans
1/4 Tsp Olive Oil
1 Lemon
Salt and Pepper to taste

Directions
1. Wash and trim the green beans and cut them on an angle in halves
2. Mix the juice of one lemon, salt, pepper and olive oil into a bowl
3. Drizzle over the cut beans and place in Air Fryer at 350 degrees for 10 to 12 minutes
4. Serve as a side to protein or on salad

LEMON HERB ROASTED POTATOES

Ingredients
1 lb Baby Potatoes
1/4 Cup Olive Oil
2 Tbsps Butter, melted
3 Cloves Garlic, minced
1 Tbsp Parsley, chopped
1 Tbsp Lemon Juice
1 Tbsp Honey
1/4 Tsp Salt
1/4 Tsp Black Pepper

Directions
1. Preheat the Air Fryer to 350 degrees
2. Cut slits on the potatoes but do not cut through
3. Mix all remaining ingredients together and brush onto the potatoes, reserving some for basting
4. Cook the in the Air Fryer for 25 minutes, then remove to baste with the oil mixture. Replace the tray and cook for a further 15 minutes until crispy
5. Serve immediately after roasting

MAPLE ROASTED PARSNIPS

Ingredients
6 Parsnips
1 Tbsp Duck or Goose Fat
1 Tbsp Dried Parsley
2 Tbsps Maple Syrup

Directions
1. Peel the parsnips and cut into one inch chunks. Place into the Air Fryer tray and drizzle with the fat
2. Cook for 35 minutes at 350 degrees
3. In the last 3 minutes of cooking, sprinkle the parsley and drizzle the maple syrup over the parsnips
4. Serve hot as a side dish

MUSHROOM KIDNEY BEAN QUINOA

Ingredients
14 Ozs Red Kidney Beans, drained and rinsed
8 Ozs Mushrooms, sliced
1 Tbsp Olive Oil
1/2 Tsp Salt
1 Tsp Pepper
8 Ozs Quinoa

Directions
1. Cook the quinoa according to package directions
2. Add the oil, mushrooms, and salt and pepper into a bowl and combine well
3. Transfer the mixture into the Air Fryer and cook at 350 degrees for 5 minutes
4. Mix the kidney beans into the cooked quinoa and add to the Air Fryer tray for another 10 minutes
5. Serve on its own or add salsa and avocado for extra nutrition

ONION RINGS

Ingredients
1 Cup Breadcrumbs
1 Tsp Chili Powder
3 Tbsps Cornflour
1 Onion
1 Cup All Purpose Flour
Salt to taste

Directions
1. Cut the onion into rings and set aside
2. In a bowl, add the flour, cornflour, salt, chili powder, and 3/4 of the breadcrumbs and mix with water to form a thick batter
3. Taking each onion ring, coat with the flour mixture and then coat with remaining breadcrumbs
4. Preheat the Air Fryer to 350 degrees
5. Place all battered rings into the Air Fryer tray and cook for 7 to 10 mins until yellow and crispy

PARMESAN ZUCCHINI CHIPS

Ingredients
2 Zucchinis
1/2 Cup Seasoned Breadcrumbs
1/2 Cup Parmesan cheese, grated
1 Beaten Egg
Cooking Spray
Salt and Pepper to season

Directions
1. Cut the zucchini into thin slices
2. Mix the cheese and breadcrumbs together then pour onto a plate
3. Toss the zucchini into the egg until well coated. Then place slices into the cheese crumb mixture and coat both sides. Finish with a coating of cooking spray
4. Put the coated zucchini chips in Air Fryer without overlapping
5. Heat the Air Fryer to 390 degrees
6. Cook in batches for 10 minutes until crispy
7. Season with salt and pepper

PLANTAIN FRITTERS

Ingredients
2 Large Plantains
1/4 Cup Onion, finely chopped
1 Cup Flour, sifted
1/4 Cup Milk
1 Tsp Vanilla Essence
2 Eggs

Directions
1. Preheat the Air Fryer to 350 degrees
2. Cut plantains into slices, ensuring that they are not too thin
3. Combine all remaining ingredients together to form a batter and whisk until well blended
4. Dip plantains into the batter, allowing the excess mixture to run off
5. Fry in the Air Fryer for 5 minutes until each side is golden brown

POTATO GRATIN

Ingredients
3 Russet Potatoes, peeled
1/4 Cup Milk
1/4 Cup Cream
1 Tsp Black Pepper
1/2 Tsp Nutmeg
1/4 Cup Gruyère Cheese, grated
* Baking Pan

Directions
1. Preheat the Air Fryer to 390 degrees
2. Slice the potatoes wafer-thin. In a bowl, mix the milk and cream and season to taste with salt, pepper and nutmeg. Coat the potato slices with the milk mixture
3. Transfer the potato slices to the pan and pour the rest of the cream mixture from the bowl on top of the potatoes. Distribute the cheese evenly over the potatoes
4. Place the pan into the Air Fryer and cook for 15 to 20 minutes until the gratin has lightly browned

POTATO STUFFED BREAD

Ingredients
4 Potatoes
6 Slices of Bread
2 Green Chilies, seeded and chopped
1 Cup Coriander, chopped
1/2 Tsp Mustard Seeds
2 Onions, chopped
1/4 Tsp Turmeric
1 Tsp Curry Powder
Cooking Spray
Salt to taste

Directions
1. Peel and boil potatoes in salted water. Once cooked through, mash them until there are no lumps
2. Coat a saucepan with cooking spray and lightly toast the mustard seeds. Mix in the curry powder, turmeric, and onions and fry until translucent
3. After a minute, add in the salt and mashed potatoes. Allow to cool
4. Shape the mix into 6 oval sized pieces
5. Trim the bread crusts off and discard. Moisten each slice with water and then press with your palm to remove excess fluid
6. Place potato stuffing in the center of each bread slice and roll until the slice is enclosed completely. They should form little football shaped pieces
7. Spray each piece so that they are evenly coated in oil
8. Preheat the Air Fryer to 390 degrees. Cook the pieces for 12 minutes until they are golden and crisp

ROAST PUMPKIN WITH STUFFING

Ingredients
Half a Butternut Pumpkin
1 Egg
1 Brown Onion
1 Carrot
2 Sweet Potatoes
3 Cloves Garlic, diced
1/2 Cup Peas
2 Tsps Mixed Herbs

Directions
1. Clean and scrape the seeds out of the pumpkin, leaving the skin intact
2. Dice the carrot, onion and sweet potatoes into even pieces
3. Combine the diced vegies, peas, mixed herbs, garlic and egg into a bowl and mix well
4. Add contents of the bowl into the pumpkin half and place in the Air Fryer for 35 minutes at 350 degrees

ROAST WINTER VEGETABLES

Ingredients
10 Ozs Parsnips
10 Ozs Celeriac
2 Red Onions
10 Ozs Butternut Squash
1 Tbsp Fresh Thyme
1 Tbsp Olive Oil
Salt and Pepper to taste

Directions
1. Preheat the Air Fryer to 390 degrees
2. Peel the parsnips, celeriac and onions. Cut the parsnips and celeriac into 2 cm cubes and the onions into wedges. Leaving the squash unpeeled, remove the seeds and cut into cubes
3. Coat the vegetables evenly with the thyme and olive oil. Season to taste
4. Place into the Air Fryer for 20 minutes and roast the vegetables until nicely brown
5. Shake the tray once during cooking to ensure even crispness

ROASTED BRUSSEL SPROUTS

Ingredients
1 lb Brussel Sprouts
1 Tbsp Olive Oil
1/2 Tsp Kosher Salt

Directions
1. Cut off the hard end of each sprout and remove any bruised outer leaves. Then cut into halves then rinse and strain until dry
2. In a bowl, toss sprouts with olive oil and kosher salt
3. Add prepared sprouts to the Air Fryer and set timer for 15 minutes at 390 degrees
4. While cooking, occasionally remove and shake the tray
5. The sprouts are done when the centers are tender and the outsides are caramelized and a bit crispy

ROASTED EGGPLANT

Ingredients
3 Medium Eggplants
1 Tbsp Soy Sauce
1 Tsp Onion Powder
1 Tsp Garlic Powder
1 Tsp Sumac
3 Tsps Za'atar
2 Bay Leaves
1/2 Lemon
1 Tsp Olive Oil

Directions
1. Wash, stem and cut the eggplant into 2cm cubes
2. Place the soy sauce, onion powder, garlic powder, sumac, za'atar and bay leaves into a bowl and coat over the eggplant cubes
3. Place the coated eggplant cubes into the Air Fryer tray and cook for 25 minutes at 350 degrees
4. In a separate bowl, mix the juice of half a lemon with the olive oil. Place the cooked eggplant in to the mixture and toss
5. Serve sprinkled with some grated cheese and fresh herbs

SEEDED BROWN LOAF

Ingredients
1/2 Cup Plain Flour
1/2 Cup Whole Wheat Flour
2 Tsps Instant Yeast
1 Tbsp Pumpkin Seeds
1 Tsp Salt
* Loaf Pan

Directions
1. In a bowl, mix all the ingredients together. Slowly add one cup (or more as needed) of lukewarm water and combine until a dough forms
2. Knead the dough for 5 minutes until it is smooth and pulls back to the touch. Shape the dough into a ball, cover in the loaf pan, and leave to rise for 20 minutes
3. Heat the Air Fryer to 390 degrees
4. Place the loaf pan into the Air Fryer and cook for 15 to 18 minutes until golden brown
5. Allow to cool before slicing

SHRIMP FRIED RICE

Ingredients
12 Prawns
5 Ozs Cooked Rice
2 Tsps Minced Garlic
10 Ozs Mixed Vegetables
3 Tbsps Shrimp Oil Paste
1/2 Cup Cilantro
1 Tbsp Soy Sauce
2 Tsps Sugar
Salt and White Pepper to taste

Directions
1. Mix the shrimp oil paste, garlic, soy sauce and sugar in a bowl
2. Peel and devein the prawns and add to the mixture
3. Place mixture with prawns into the Air Fryer for 7 minutes at 390 degrees
4. Add the cooked rice and vegetables into the tray and stir through. Cook for a further 7 minutes
5. Remove fried rice and garnish with cilantro. Season with additional salt or white pepper to taste

SMASHED FINGERLING POTATOES

Ingredients
1 lb Fingerling Potatoes
2 Garlic Cloves, minced
1/3 Cup Parsley, diced
Salt and Pepper to season
1/2 Tbsp Butter

Directions
1. Wash the potatoes. Leaving the peel on, boil in salted water for 13 minutes
2. Once cooled, flatten each potato using a spatula whilst allowing it to retain shape
3. Heat the Air Fryer to 350 degrees
4. Place smashed potatoes into the Air Fryer tray and cook for 25 minutes. Shake the tray and resume cooking for another 7 minutes for additional crispness
5. Under medium heat, add the garlic, diced parsley, and butter into a pan until fragrant
6. Add potatoes into the pan for another minute so that they are well coated
7. Serve whilst hot and season with salt and pepper

SPICY PARSNIP CHIPS

Ingredients
2 Parsnips, peeled into ribbons
1 ½ Tsps Salt
1/2 Tsp Grated Orange Rind
1/2 Tsp Hot Chili Flakes
1/4 Tsp Ground Cumin

Directions
1. To make a chili salt, combine the sea salt, orange rind, chili flakes and cumin in a small bowl
2. Preheat the Air Fryer to 350 degrees
3. Cook the parsnip ribbons in the Air Fryer tray for 2 minutes or until crisp and golden
4. Sprinkle with chili salt to serve

STUFFED MUSHROOMS WITH SOUR CREAM

Ingredients
24 Mushrooms, stalks removed
2 Rashers Bacon
1/2 Onion
1/2 Capsicum
1 Carrot
1 Cup Grated Cheese
1/2 Cup Sour Cream
Extra Cheese to top

Directions
1. Finely chop the bacon, onion, capsicum, carrots and mushroom stalks
2. Sauté the diced bacon and vegetables in a pan until all ingredients are soft
3. Stir in the sour cream and cheese then continue to heat until the cheese has melted
4. Spoon a heaping of the stuffing into each mushroom head and sprinkle with a little cheese
5. Add the mushrooms into the Air Fryer tray and cook for 8 minutes at 350 degrees

STUFFED PEPPERS

Ingredients
6 Capsicums
1/3 Cups Grated Parmesan Cheese
3 Cloves Garlic, finely chopped
2 Tsps Mixed Herbs
1 Carrot
1 Onion
1 Potato
1 Bread Roll
1/2 Cup Peas

Directions
1. Cut the tops off the capsicums and remove all the seeds and white pith using a spoon
2. Dice the carrot, onion, potato and bread roll into equal sized pieces
3. Add the diced capsicum, vegetables, bread and garlic to a bowl. Add the peas and herb mix then combine thoroughly
4. Preheat the Air Fryer to 350 degrees
5. Fill the capsicums with the filling then place into the Air Fryer and cook for 20 minutes
6. Open the tray and add the grated cheese over each pepper. Cook for another 5 minutes

STUFFED PORTOBELLO MUSHROOMS

Ingredients
3 Portobello Mushrooms
1 Green Pepper, diced
1 Tomato, diced
2 Slices Ham, chopped
1 Tsp Garlic, minced
1 Red Onion, diced
Grated Cheddar or Mozzarella Cheese
1/2 Tsp Salt
Pinch of Black Pepper
1 Tbsp Olive Oil

Directions
1. Preheat the Air Fryer to 320 degrees
2. Remove the mushroom stems, wash and pat dry. Drizzle olive oil all over mushrooms until they are well coated
3. Combine green pepper, ham, tomato, garlic, onion, salt, black pepper and cheese in a large bowl
4. Spoon the mixture into each mushroom cap. Top with more cheese if desired
5. Place filled caps into Air Fryer for 8 minutes until top is brown and cheese is melted
6. Serve as a side or with eggs

SWEET POTATO FRIES

Ingredients
2 Sweet Potatoes
1 Tbsp Olive Oil
Salt to taste

Directions
1. Wash and peel the potatoes. Cut into either fries or chips depending on preference and place in a bowl
2. Pour the oil over the potato and toss until it is well coated
3. Place fries into the Air Fryer tray and cook at 320 degrees for 16 minutes. Toss the tray once during cooking to ensure that they are even and crisp
4. After 16 minutes, raise the temperature to 350 degrees and cook for a further 4 minutes
5. Season with salt and serve piping hot

SNACKS

ASIAN ROASTED CHICKEN WINGS

Ingredients
1 lb Chicken Wings
2 Cloves Garlic
2 Tsps Ginger Powder
1 Tsp Ground Cumin
Salt and White Pepper to taste
1/2 Cup Sweet Chili Sauce

Directions
1. Mix the garlic with the ginger powder, cumin, white pepper and salt. Rub the chicken wings into this mixture to coat
2. Put the chicken wings into the Air Fryer for 18 minutes at 350 degrees until they are crispy and cooked through
3. Serve with the chili sauce

BACON WRAPPED SHRIMP

Ingredients
1 lb Tiger Shrimp, peeled and deveined
1 lb Bacon Slices

Directions
1. Take one slice of bacon and wrap it around the shrimp, starting from the head and finishing at the tail. Return the wrapped shrimp to the refrigerator for 20 minutes
2. Preheat the Air Fryer to 350 degrees
3. Remove the shrimp from the refrigerator and add half of them to the cooking tray, cooking each batch for 5 to 7 minutes
4. Drain on a paper towel prior to serving

BAJA FISH TACOS

Ingredients
1 lb Cod Fillets
6 Tomatoes, diced
1 Onion, diced
1/2 Cup Cilantro, chopped
2 Tbsps Jalapeno Peppers, diced
1/2 Tsp Garlic Salt
1/2 Lime
9 Ozs Batter Mix
1 Can of Mexican Beer
24 Corn Tortillas
2 Cups Shredded Mexican Cheese Blend
2 Limes, wedged
1 Dash Chile-Garlic Sauce

Directions
1. Mix tomatoes, onion, cilantro, jalapeno peppers, and garlic salt in a bowl. Squeeze 1/2 lime over the salsa fresca. Cover bowl with plastic wrap and refrigerate while preparing fish
2. Preheat the Air Fryer to 340 degrees
3. Stir batter mix and beer together in a bowl
4. Cut the cod into 2 inch chunks and dip into the batter mix
5. Place battered cod into the Air Fryer tray and cook in batches for 5 minutes until golden brown
6. Microwave corn tortillas until warmed for about 1 minute
7. Stack two tortillas on a plate; top with fish, a sprinkle of Mexican cheese, salsa fresca, and a squeeze from lime wedge. Drizzle with chile-garlic sauce to serve

BANANA CHIPS

Ingredients
3 Bananas
1 Lemon
1/2 Cup Water

Directions
1. Peel and cut bananas into 1/4 inch thick slices
2. Juice the lemon and mix this with the water
3. Soak the banana slices in this mixture for 10 minutes to avoid browning
4. Preheat the Air Fryer at 350 degrees
5. Add slices into the tray and fry the chips for 15 minutes
6. Serve immediately or store chips in an airtight jar (lasts for 1 to 2 weeks)

BASIL RICOTTA BALLS

Ingredients
1/2 lb Ricotta
2 Tbsps Flour
1 Egg, separated
Salt and Black Pepper
2 Tsps Basil, finely chopped
1 Tbsp Chives, finely chopped
3 Slices Stale Bread

Directions
1. Combine the ricotta in a bowl with the flour, egg yolk, salt and pepper. Stir the basil and chives through the mixture
2. Divide the mixture into 15 equal portions and shape them into balls with wet hands. Allow to rest for 10 minutes
3. Grind the bread slices into fine breadcrumbs in a food processor and mix with the olive oil. Pour the mixture into a deep dish. Briefly beat the egg white in another deep dish
4. Preheat the Air Fryer to 390 degrees
5. Carefully coat the ricotta balls in the egg white and then in the breadcrumbs
6. Put half the balls in the Air Fryer for 8 minutes. Bake the balls until golden brown. Repeat with remaining balls
7. Serve with sweet chili sauce

BEEF AND FETA RICE BALLS

Ingredients
1 lb Ground Beef
1 Onion, finely chopped
4 Garlic Cloves, minced
3 Cups Cooked Rice
4 Eggs (3 beaten, 1 whole)
1/3 Cup Butter, melted
1/2 Cup Grated Parmesan Cheese
Pinch of Cayenne Pepper
2 Tbsps Dried Parsley
1/2 Cup Crumbled Feta Cheese
1 Tsp Garlic Powder
Salt and Pepper to taste
1 Cup Breadcrumbs

Directions
1. In a skillet, cook the ground beef with onion and garlic until browned. Drain the fat then transfer to a bowl to cool
2. Add in the rice, 2/3 of the beaten eggs, butter, both cheese, cayenne pepper and parsley. Mix to combine, then season with salt and pepper and some garlic powder. Chill the mixture for at least 2 hours or overnight
3. Shape the mixture into about 1-1/2 inch balls
4. Place the remaining beaten egg into a bowl and the breadcrumbs into another bowl
5. Dip each rice ball into the egg then coat in the breadcrumb mix
6. Preheat the Air Fryer to 390 degrees
7. Fry the balls in the Air Fryer tray until golden brown for about 4 to 5 minutes

BEEF AND VEGETABLE MEATBALLS

Ingredients
1 lb Beef Mince
1 Carrot
1 Zucchini
1 Onion
2 Cloves Garlic
1 Tsp Dried Oregano
1 Egg
3/4 Cup Breadcrumbs
Salt and Pepper to taste
1 Cup Plain Flour
Olive Oil

Directions
1. Chop the carrot, zucchini, onion and garlic in a food processor
2. In a large bowl, combine the mince, oregano, egg, breadcrumbs, salt, pepper and the vegetable mix
3. Roll the mixture into even balls and refrigerate for 30 minutes or until you are ready to use them
4. Preheat the Air Fryer to 350 degrees
5. Start to roll the balls into the flour gently. Once coated, place the balls into the Air Fryer tray and cook for 15 to 20 minutes turning occasionally until they are golden
6. Repeat until all meatballs are cooked

BEEF CHILI

Ingredients
1 lb Lean Ground Beef
1 Onion, chopped
1 Red Pepper, chopped
2 Hot Chili Peppers, seeded and chopped
1 Tbsp Olive Oil
2 Tbsps Tomato Paste
1 ½ Cups Beef Broth
1 Tsp Ground Cumin
1 Tsp Coriander
1 Can Diced Tomatoes
1 Can Kidney Beans, drained and rinsed
Salt and Pepper to taste

Directions
1. Place the oil, onion, red pepper and hot chili peppers in the Air Fryer tray. Cook for 5 minutes at 350 degrees
2. Add the beef into the tray and cook for 6 minutes or until the meat is browned all over
3. Whisk the tomato paste with 1/2 cup of broth, cumin and coriander. Add the broth mixture and diced tomatoes to the Air Fryer. Cook for 20 minutes
4. Add the kidney beans and remaining broth to the tray. Cook for 10 minutes or until beans are heated through
5. Season to taste with salt and pepper

BLACK-EYED PEA AND HAM BITES

Ingredients
1 Cup Cooked Ham, chopped
1 Can Black-Eyed Peas, drained and mashed
2 Shallots, chopped
1/2 Red Bell Pepper, chopped
1 Cup Cornstarch
4 Egg Whites
Salt and Black Pepper

Directions
1. In a large bowl, combine the peas, shallot, bell pepper and ham. Mix in cornstarch, egg whites, and some salt and pepper, to taste. The mixture should be a soft doughy consistency
2. Take individual spoons of the mixture and roll into small balls. Place balls into the refrigerator for 30 minutes to retain shape
3. Preheat the Air Fryer to 350 degrees
4. Place balls into the Air Fryer tray and cook for 6 minutes until golden brown and crispy
5. Serve with cranberry or tomato sauce

BLOOMING ONION

Ingredients
Large Sweet Onion
1 Egg
1 Cup Whole Milk
1 Cup All Purpose Flour
1 ½ Tsps Salt
1 ½ Tsps Cayenne Pepper
1 Tsp Paprika
1/2 Tsp Black Pepper
1/3 Tsp Dried Oregano
1/8 Tsp Dried Thyme
1/8 Tsp Ground Cumin
1/2 Cup Spicy Sauce

Directions
1. Whisk the egg and milk together in a bowl
2. In another bowl, mix remaining ingredients (except for the onion) until well combined
3. To prepare the onion, remove the skin and then cut off the bottom and top. Use a sharp and narrow knife to remove a half inch core from the center of the onion. Once the core is removed, cut slits down into the onion (but do not slice to the very bottom) until you have even formed slices
4. Bend the slices downwards to form the appearance of petals
5. Place the onion into the egg and milk mix, then add into the seasoned flour mixture. Do this twice until there is a thick coating on each petal
6. Preheat the Air Fryer to 350 degrees
7. Place the battered onion into the Air Fryer tray and cook for 8 minutes or until crispy
8. Serve with a spicy sauce poured into the center of the fried onion

BUFFALO CHICKEN EGG ROLLS

Ingredients
3 Chicken Breasts, cooked and shredded
1/2 Cup Hot Sauce
8 Ozs Cream Cheese
3 Ozs Blue Cheese
50 Wonton Wrappers

Directions
1. Combine the shredded chicken, cream cheese, and hot sauce in a bowl
2. Lay out wonton wrappers on a clean dry surface. Fill the wonton wrappers with a teaspoon of the chicken mixture. Be sure to have the mixture on one corner of the wonton wrapper instead of in the center or spread all over the wonton
3. Add a large crumble of blue cheese to the chicken mixture. Fold the outside corners to the center over the filling. Pull the corner closest to the filling mixture over the mixture so that it meets the other two corners
4. Roll up the chicken egg roll tightly, but not so tight the filling squishes out. Wet the final edge to secure well
5. Repeat with remaining wonton wrappers and filling
6. Heat the Air Fryer to 375 degrees
7. Place the egg rolls into the Air Fryer tray in batches. Allow to cook for 5 minutes until all sides are golden brown
8. Serve with ranch dip

BUTTERFLIED SHRIMP

Ingredients
1 lb Large Shrimp, peeled and butterflied
1 Quart Water
1½ Cups Cornstarch
5 Cups Breadcrumbs
2 Eggs

Directions
1. Preheat the Air Fryer to 350 degrees
2. In a large bowl, pour in water and mix in cornstarch and eggs
3. Dip the shrimp into the mixture allowing them to be completely coated. Then roll the shrimp in the breadcrumbs and coat well. Repeat this process twice on each shrimp for thicker coating
4. Place shrimp into the Air Fryer tray and cook for 8 minutes until they are golden brown

BUTTERMILK CHICKEN

Ingredients
3 Chicken Breasts
3 Chicken Legs
3 Cups Buttermilk
2 Cups Plain Flour
4 Eggs, beaten
2 ½ Cups Cornmeal
1 Tbsp Paprika
Salt and Pepper to taste

Directions
1. Thoroughly clean the chicken and place dried pieces into a bowl. Sprinkle with salt and pepper, then immerse with the buttermilk. Cover the bowl with cling film and place in the fridge to marinate overnight
2. Preheat the Air Fryer to 350 degrees
3. Place the beaten eggs and flour into 2 bowls. Season the cornmeal with paprika, salt and pepper and place into another bowl
4. Take marinated chicken out of the fridge and dip each piece in flour, then into the eggs, and then coat evenly with the seasoned cornmeal. Repeat the process for additional crispness
5. Place chicken pieces into the Air Fryer tray and cook for 20 to 25 minutes
6. Serve immediately

CAJIN SHRIMP

Ingredients
1/2 lb Tiger Shrimp
1/4 Tsp Cayenne Pepper
1/2 Tsp Old Bay Seasoning
1/4 Tsp Smoked Paprika
1 Pinch Salt
1 Tbsp Olive Oil

Directions
1. Heat the Air Fryer to 390 degrees
2. In a mixing bowl, combine all of the ingredients, coating the shrimp with the oil and the spices
3. Place the shrimp into the Air Fryer and cook for 5 minutes
4. Serve with steamed vegetables or over rice

CARAMELIZED CHESTNUTS

Ingredients
1 lb Whole Chestnuts
1 Cup Icing Sugar
1 Tbsp Salt

Directions
1. Preheat the Air Fryer to 350 degrees
2. In a large bowl, sift together the sugar and salt. Add chestnuts to the mixture, tossing gently to coat
3. Place coated chestnuts into the Air Fryer and cook for 12 minutes until the mixture has caramelized
4. Allow to cool before serving

CATFISH NUGGETS

Ingredients
2 lbs Catfish Fillets
2 Tbsps Dried Thyme
1 Cup Mustard
2 Cups All Purpose Flour
1 Tsp Salt
1 Tsp Black Pepper
1 Tsp Baking Soda

Directions
1. Cut the fillets into 1 ½ inch pieces
2. Place the catfish pieces into a mixing bowl and sprinkle with thyme leaves. Mix in the mustard with your hands. Cover and refrigerate overnight
3. Preheat the Air Fryer to 340 degrees
4. Whisk the flour, salt, black pepper, and baking soda together in a mixing bowl
5. Dip the catfish pieces one at a time into the flour mixture and shake off the excess
6. Fry the catfish nuggets for 3 to 4 minutes in batches until they are no longer translucent and are golden brown

CELERY PRAWNS

Ingredients
6 Stalks of Celery, sliced diagonally
1/2 Carrot, sliced
10 Prawns
3 Cloves Minced Garlic
1 Tbsp Oyster Sauce
2 Tsps Soy Sauce
1 Tsp Sugar
1 Tsp Cornstarch
1 Cup Water

Directions
1. Put garlic, celery and carrot into the Air Fryer and cook for 7 minutes at 350 degrees
2. Mix the oyster sauce, soy sauce, sugar, cornstarch and water in a bowl. Add the mixture into the Air Fryer for 2 minutes
3. Add in the prawns and cook for another 5 minutes until mixture has thickened
4. Once done, transfer to a plate and serve with rice

CHEESE AND BACON BREAD BAKE

Ingredients
10 Ozs Bacon, diced
6 Eggs
1¼ Cups Milk
1/4 Tsp Salt
Kosher Salt
Black Pepper
7 Cups Baguette, cut into 2cm cubes
2 Cups Grated Cheddar Cheese
1 Tbsp Parsley, finely chopped
Cooking Spray
* Round Cake Tin

Directions
1. Heat a pan over high heat. Add the bacon to the pan and cook until lightly browned. Remove from the fry pan and drain on a paper towel
2. Whisk the eggs, milk, salt and pepper in a bowl
3. Place the cubed bread in a large zip lock bag. Pour in the egg mixture, 1½ cups of cheese and cooked bacon. Seal and massage the egg into the bread. Set aside in the fridge for at least 30 minutes
4. Preheat the Air Fryer at 350 degrees
5. Lightly coat the cake tin with the cooking spray. Pour the bread mixture into the tin, pat down to compress and scatter with remaining cheese
6. Place the cake tin into the Air Fryer and bake for 30 minutes until bubbly and golden on top
7. Allow to cool slightly before slicing. Garnish with parsley to serve

CHEESE CORN AND SPINACH SQUARES

Ingredients

For the Stuffing:
1/2 Cup Sweet Corn
2 Tbsps Spinach, boiled and chopped
1/2 Tsp Garlic, finely chopped
2 Tbsps Mozzarella Cheese
1 Onion, chopped
2 Tbsps Grated Parmesan Cheese
Salt to taste
1 Tbsp Bread crumbs
1/2 Tsp Black pepper
Pinch of Nutmeg

For the Pastry:
1 Cup All Purpose Flour
Pinch of Baking Powder
Salt to taste
1 Tsp Chili Flakes
1/4 Tsp Dried Basil
1 Cup Buttermilk

Directions
1. In a bowl, add in all the ingredients for the stuffing, mix well and keep aside
2. To make the pastry, combine the flour, baking powder, salt, chili flakes and basil in a bowl and mix. Gradually add the buttermilk into the mixture and knead into a soft dough. Allow to rest for 30 minutes in the fridge whilst covered in cling film
3. Once the dough has been rested, dust some flour on a clean surface and roll the dough into a thin sheet. Cut into palm sized squares
4. Spoon in the stuffing on one side of the square. Brush some water on the edges of the square, fold and seal the pastry

5. In a bowl, make a thin mixture of flour and water and keep aside. Dip the stuffed pastry into this, then remove and coat with breadcrumbs
6. Preheat the Air Fryer at 350 degrees
7. Place the squares in the tray and fry them for 5 minutes. After few minutes, open the tray and brush them with little oil on both sides and re-fry for another 2 to 3 minutes
8. Serve with tomato sauce

CHEESE CRACKERS

Ingredients
2 Cups Grated Cheddar Cheese
1/4 Cup Butter, softened
1 Cup Flour
1/2 Tsp Salt
2 Tbsps Milk

Directions
1. Preheat the Air Fryer to 350 degrees
2. Place the cheese, butter, flour, and salt into a food processor. Pulse until the dough forms coarse crumbs
3. Slowly add the milk, 1 tablespoon at a time, with the food processor on, until the dough becomes a ball
4. Divide the dough into two balls and refrigerate for 15 minutes. Remove one dough ball from the refrigerator, and roll it on a floured board with a rolling pin until it is about 1/8 inch thick
5. Cut the dough into 1 inch squares with a sharp knife. Use a toothpick to poke a hole in the center of each cracker
6. Place the crackers into the Air Fryer, ensuring that they do not overlap. You may need to cook in batches
7. Cook for 12 to 15 minutes until the edges are just starting to brown and the cracker is starting to puff
8. Remove and allow to cool. Eat or store in a covered container for up to 3 days

CHEESE MOCHI BALLS

Ingredients
1/2 Cup Rice Flour
1/2 Cup Milk
1/4 Cup Cheese
1/2 Tbsp Vegetable Oil

Directions
1. Add all ingredients into a food processor and blend until the mixture becomes dough
2. Roll the dough into small even balls and place them in the Air Fryer tray
3. Bake for 12 to 14 minutes at 300 degrees until the balls are crispy to touch

CHEESE-STEAK EGG ROLLS

Ingredients
9 Ozs Steak Strips
10 Egg Roll Wrappers
1/2 Bell Pepper, diced
1/2 Onion, diced
3 Tbsps Butter
1 Tsp Garlic Powder
5 Slices Cheddar Cheese, cut into halves
1 Egg, whisked

For the Sauce:
1/2 Cup Mayonnaise
3 Tsps Milk
1 Tsp Horseradish
1/4 Tsp Garlic Powder
Black Pepper to season

Directions
1. Over a medium flame, cook the butter, onion and bell pepper until tender. Mix in the garlic powder and steak strips and allow to cook for another 5 minutes. Cool the mixture
2. Assemble the wrappers on a clean benchtop and line the edges with the egg. Position two strips of the steak mix onto the wrapper, then place a piece of cheddar cheese on top. Fold the wrapper ends together to enclose and form a roll
3. Place the egg rolls into the Air Fryer tray in batches at 390 degrees. Allow to cook for 5 to 7 minutes until crispy and slightly browned
4. Mix together all ingredients for the sauce and serve with cooked egg rolls

CHICKEN AND CREAM CHEESE PASTRIES

Ingredients
1 Chicken Breast
2 Tsps Olive Oil
1 Onion, chopped
3 Garlic Cloves, minced
2 Tsps Dried Oregano
1/4 Tsp Chili Powder
2 Ozs Cream Cheese
2 Sheets Puff Pastry

Directions
1. Under a medium flame, cook the chicken in a pan and immerse with water to simmer. Remove the pan, cover with a lid, and leave for 18 minutes to poach the breast. Once cooked through, allow to cool and finely shred the meat
2. In another pan, heat the olive oil and cook the garlic and onion until softened. Add the shredded chicken, oregano, cream cheese and chili for a further minute and then allow to cool
3. Using the head of a round bowl, cut out 8 circles from the puff pastry sheets
4. Take a tablespoon of the chicken mixture and place into the center of each circle. Moisten the edges of the pastry and fold the circle in half to enclose the mix. Press the ends with a fork to secure
5. Heat the Air Fryer to 350 degrees
6. Place pasties into the Air Fryer tray and cook for 3 to 4 minutes until crispy
7. Serve with side salad and chili sauce

CHICKEN NUGGETS

Ingredients
4 Chicken Breasts
4 Cups Flour
5 Tbsps Garlic Salt
3 Tbsps Black Pepper
4 Eggs, whisked

Directions
1. Cut the chicken breasts into even bite sized pieces
2. Preheat the Air Fryer to 350 degrees
3. In a large bowl, combine the garlic salt, black pepper and flour
4. Place the eggs into a shallow bowl and coat each chicken piece well. Once covered in egg, coat with the seasoned flour ensuring that all sides are well covered
5. Cook the chicken nuggets in the Air Fryer for 10 minutes. Shake the tray and reinsert, then cook for a further 8 minutes until browned and crispy
6. Serve with your choice of sauce

CHILEAN FRIED CALZONES

Ingredients
1 ½ Cups Plain Flour
6 Tbsps Icing Sugar
1 ½ Tsps Brandy or Cognac
1 Egg and 1 Egg Yolk
1 ½ Tsps Baking Powder
Zest of 1 Lemon
2 Tbsps Butter, melted
1/4 Tsp Salt

Directions
1. Preheat the Air Fryer to 375 degrees
2. In a large bowl, combine the salt, baking powder, sugar, and plain flour
3. Combine the butter, liquor, eggs and lemon zest in a separate bowl and pour into the flour mix. Knead the ingredients together until it forms a smooth dough
4. Dust a clean work surface with flour and roll the dough until it is a quarter of an inch in thickness
5. Take a knife and slice the dough into 2 x 4.5 inch pieces. Then cut a small slit lengthways into each piece and pull the end of each rectangle into the hole, flatten slightly with your hand to ensure that the pastry shape is secured
6. Place the calzones into the Air Fryer tray and cook for 2 or more minutes until crispy
7. Dust fried calzones with icing sugar to serve

CHILI CHICKPEA BITES

Ingredients
1 Can Chickpeas
1 Tbsp Olive Oil
1 Tsp Chili Powder
1 Tsp Salt

Directions
1. Drain the can of chick peas and rinse under water. Place on several paper towels and dry well
2. Mix all ingredients together and add to Air Fryer for 20 minutes at 350 degrees. Shake the tray once during cooking process to ensure that all chickpeas become crisp
3. Remove and serve

CHILI TUNA PUFFS

Ingredients
1/2 Cup Chili Tuna
1 Sheet Puff Pastry

Directions
1. Preheat the Air Fryer to 375 degrees
2. Thaw the pastry and cut into 4 equal squares
3. Spoon the chili tuna into the center of each square pastry
4. Fold the pastry to form a triangle or a rectangle and seal the edges together by pressing the down with a fork
5. Place the pastries into the Air Fryer tray and allow to bake for 10 to 12 minutes until they turn golden brown

CHINESE WONTONS

Ingredients
1 lb Ground Pork
3 Minced Garlic Cloves
1 Tsp Grated Ginger
1 Tbsp Soy Sauce
1 Tsp Sesame Oil
3 Carrots, diced
3 Stalks Celery, diced
6 Green Onions, diced
12 Oz Pack Wonton Wrappers

Directions
1. Combine pork, garlic, ginger, soy sauce, and vegetables in a bowl
2. Place a spoonful of filling in the center of each wonton wrapper. Brush water on 2 borders of the skin, covering 1/4 inch from the edge. Fold skin over to form a triangle, sealing the wonton intact
3. Heat the Air Fryer to 390 degrees. Place wontons into the tray in batches and cook for 10 minutes until crispy and golden
4. Drain and serve with chili sauce

CHORIZO EMPANADES

Ingredients
5 Ozs Chorizo, cubed
1 Shallot, finely chopped
1/4 Cup Red Bell Pepper, cubed
2 Tbsps Parsley
7 Ozs Chilled Pizza Dough

Directions
1. Stir the chorizos, shallots and bell peppers in a pan on low heat for 2 to 3 minutes until the bell pepper is tender. Take off the heat and stir in the parsley. Allow the mixture to cool
2. Preheat the Air Fryer to 390 degrees
3. Use a glass to cut twenty 5cm rounds from the dough. Scoop a spoonful of the chorizo mixture onto each round. Press the edges together between your fingers to create a scallop pattern
4. Put empanadas into the Air Fryer for 10 minutes and cook until golden brown. You may need to do this in batches
5. Serve when golden brown and crisp

CLAM FRITTERS

Ingredients
1 Cup Minced Clams
1 Cup All Purpose Flour
2 Tsps Baking Powder
1 Egg
Black Pepper to taste

Directions
1. Preheat the Air Fryer to 350 degrees
2. Whisk the flour and baking powder together in a bowl
3. Beat the egg in a separate bowl until smooth. Stir in the minced clams and black pepper to taste. Stir in the flour to form a batter
4. Take spoonfuls of the batter and form into small rounded fritters. Continue until all batter is used up. Then place fritters on a tray and freeze for 5 minutes to retain the shape
5. Place the fritters into the Air Fryer tray and cook for about 4 minutes until golden

CORN DOGS

Ingredients
12 Ozs Hot Dogs
1/2 Cup Plain Flour
2 Tbsps Sugar
2 Tsps Baking Powder
3/4 Cup Yellow Cornmeal
1/4 Tsp Salt
1/2 Cup Milk
1 Egg
* Bamboo Skewers

Directions
1. Cut each hot dog in half and poke a skewer into the sliced end of each sausage
2. Combine the milk, cornmeal, egg, plain flour, baking powder and salt in a bowl and mix well
3. Preheat the Air Fryer to 350 degrees
4. Holding the skewer end, place each hot dog into the mixture and coat evenly
5. Place the corn dogs into the Air Fryer and allow to cook for 4 minutes or until the batter is brown and crispy
6. Serve with ketchup and mustard

CORN TORTILLA CHIPS

Ingredients
8 Corn Tortillas
1 Tbsp Olive Oil
Salt to taste

Directions
1. Cut corn tortillas into bite sized triangles
2. Brush with olive oil so that each piece is lightly coated
3. Preheat the Air Fryer to 390 degrees and place tortilla pieces into the tray for 3 minutes until crispy
4. Sprinkle with salt and serve. Add chili flakes for an added flavor kick

CRAB AND FENNEL WONTONS

Ingredients
1/2 lb Crab Meat
1 Cup Fennel, diced
1 Tbsp Honey
Juice of 1 Lime
1/4 Cup Chopped Chives
4 Dashes Hot Pepper Sauce
1/2 Tbsp Olive Oil
1 Pack Square Wonton Skins
1 Egg, beaten
Salt and White Pepper to taste

Directions
1. In a large bowl, mix crabmeat, diced fennel, honey, lime juice, chives, hot pepper sauce and olive oil
2. Spoon a small amount of filling on each wonton wrapper and brush edges with egg. Fold wontons in half into triangles and secure the corners
3. Preheat the Air Fryer to 350 degrees
4. Cook wontons in the Air Fryer tray for 10 minutes or until golden brown
5. Serve with soy sauce

CRAB CAKES

Ingredients
1 lb Crabmeat
1 Egg, beaten
2 Tsps Mustard
1 Tsp Worcestershire Sauce
Juice of 1 Lemon
1 Tsp Chili Sauce
1/2 Tsp Old Bay Seasoning
1/2 Cup Red Bell Pepper, chopped
1 Scallion, chopped
3/4 Cup Breadcrumbs
1/4 Tsp Salt
Black Pepper to taste

Directions
1. Preheat the Air Fryer to 390 degrees
2. Mix together the bell pepper, egg, scallion, mustard, Worcestershire sauce, lemon juice, Old Bay seasoning and chili sauce
3. Add in a quarter of the breadcrumbs and the crabmeat. Season with salt and pepper
4. Portion the mixture into eight even pieces. Roll into a ball and flatten into a patty shape with your palm
5. Place each crab cake into the remaining breadcrumbs and coat well
6. Cook crab cakes in the Air Fryer for 6 to 8 minutes until crisp
7. Serve with tartare or cocktail sauce

CRAB CROQUETTES

Ingredients
For the Filling:
1 lb Crab Meat
2 Egg Whites, beaten
1 Tbsp Olive Oil
1/4 Cup Red Onion, finely chopped
1/4 Red Bell Pepper, finely chopped
2 Tbsps Celery, finely chopped
1/4 Tsp Tarragon, finely chopped
1/2 Tsp Parsley, finely chopped
1/2 Tsp Cayenne Pepper
1/4 Cup Mayonnaise
1/4 Cup Sour Cream

For the Breading:
3 Eggs, beaten
1 Cup All Purpose Flour
1 Cup Panko Breadcrumbs
1 Tsp Olive Oil
1/2 Tsp Salt

Directions
1. In a pan, cook the olive oil, onions, peppers, and celery. Sauté until translucent for about 4 to 5 minutes. Remove from heat and set aside to cool
2. In a food processor, blend the breadcrumbs, olive oil and salt to a fine crumb. Prepare the beaten eggs, panko mixture and flour on individual bowls
3. To form the crab mixture, combine the crab meat, mayonnaise, sour cream, spices, egg whites, and vegetables in a bowl
4. Mold crab mixture into small balls. Roll each ball in the flour, then in the beaten eggs and finally in panko
5. Preheat the Air Fryer to 390 degrees
6. Place croquettes into the Air Fryer tray and ensure that they do not overlap

7. Cook each batch for 8 to 10 minutes or until golden brown

CRANBERRY MEATBALLS

Ingredients
1 lb Minced Beef
4 Garlic Cloves, finely diced
1/2 Cup Parmesan Cheese, shredded
2 Tsps Italian Seasoning
2 Tsps Parsley, diced
Salt and Pepper to season
1 Cup Panko Breadcrumbs
1/3 Cup Cranberry Sauce
1/2 Cup Barbecue Sauce
1 Egg

Directions
1. Preheat the Air Fryer to 390 degrees
2. Mix together the beef, parmesan, parsley, Italian seasoning, garlic, egg, salt, pepper and panko. Gradually add a quarter cup of warm water to the mixture and combine well
3. Take a large spoonful of meat and roll into medium sized balls. Continue rolling until the mixture is finished
4. Place balls into the Air Fryer and cook for 18 minutes until done
5. In the meanwhile, pour the barbecue and cranberry sauce into a pan over a medium flame. Keep cooking until the two sauces dissolve together
6. Pour sauce over cook meatballs to serve

CREPE WRAPPED PRAWNS

Ingredients
9 Ozs Prawns
1 Tsp Cornflour
1 Pinch of Sugar
1 Tsps Vinegar
1/2 Tsp Minced Garlic
1/2 Tsp Minced Ginger
1/2 Tsp Soya Sauce
1/2 Tsp Chili Flakes
1 Tsp Chili Sauce
1 Tsp Butter
2 Tbsp Breadcrumbs
1 Packet Spring Roll Sheets

Directions
1. In a bowl, add the prawns, corn flour, sugar, vinegar, garlic, ginger, soya sauce, chili flakes, chili sauce, and mix well
2. Take a spring roll sheet and apply the butter on top. Sprinkle some breadcrumbs on top and cut into thin strips
3. Take two strips and wrap around each prawn
4. Preheat the Air Fryer to 375 degrees
5. Place the wrapped prawns in the Air Fryer tray and cook 7 minutes until brown and crispy
6. Remove and serve hot with a cocktail sauce

CRISP SPICY TUNA SUSHI

Ingredients
5 Ozs Sashimi Grade Tuna
2 Green Onions
1 Tsp Sugar
1 Tsp Chili Sauce
2 Tsp Japanese Mayonnaise
4 Cups Cooked Rice
3 Tbsps Rice Vinegar
Cooking Spray
*1 x Bamboo Sushi Mat

Directions
1. To make sushi rice, combine cooked rice with vinegar and sugar. Mix thoroughly
2. Slice the tuna lengthwise into small pieces
3. Position the rice onto the bamboo sushi mat lined with plastic wrap
4. Layer the tuna pieces down the center of the rice. Top with chili sauce and mayonnaise
5. Roll, squeeze and mold rice into a long even column. Ensure that it is tightly packed
6. Wet a knife and cut the sushi column into nigiri slices
7. Place the pieces into the Air Fryer for 13 minutes at 390 degrees
8. Serve with wasabi and soy

CRISPY BOCCONCINI

Ingredients
2 Tbsps Flour
2 Eggs
1 ¼ Cups Panko Breadcrumbs
1/4 Cup Parmesan Cheese, grated
8 Ozs Baby Bocconcini Cheese
Chili Sauce to serve

Directions
1. Whisk the egg and set aside. Mix together the panko and parmesan cheese on a plate. Add the flour to another plate
2. Taking each bocconcini, coat in the flour, then in the whisked egg, and finally in the panko mixture. Do this twice for additional crispness. Place coated bocconcini into the freezer for 15 minutes to firm
3. Preheat the Air Fryer to 320 degrees
4. Place the bocconcini into the Air Fryer tray and cook for 3 minutes or until lightly browned
5. Serve with chili sauce

CRISPY CHICKEN WONTONS

Ingredients
14 Ozs Minced Chicken
50 Wonton wrappers
1 Green Onion, minced
1 ½ Tbsps Soy Sauce
1 Tbsp Sesame Oil
1 Tbsp Vegetable Oil
1/4 Tsp Salt
1 Egg

Directions
1. Mix the chicken, egg, green onion, soy sauce, sesame oil, vegetable oil, and salt in a large bowl until evenly combined
2. Scoop a small spoon of the chicken mixture and place into the center of a wonton wrapper
3. Moisten adjacent edges of the wrapper with water and fold into a triangle. Connect the two lower points of the wrapper and moisten to seal and make a hat shape. Repeat with remaining chicken and wonton wrappers
4. Preheat the Air Fryer at 350 degrees
5. Place the wontons in the Air Fryer to fry for 22 minutes until crispy
6. Serve with preferred sauce

CRISPY HOT PRAWNS WITH COCKTAIL SAUCE

Ingredients
12 Large Tiger Prawns
1 Tsp Chili Flakes
1 Tsp Chili Powder
1/2 Tsp Salt
1/2 Tsp Black Pepper
3 Tbsps Mayonnaise
1 Tbsp Ketchup
1 Tbsp Cider

Directions
1. In a medium bowl, combine the salt, pepper, chili powder and chili flakes. Peel and devein the prawns, then coat them in the mixture
2. Heat the Air Fryer to 375 degrees
3. Place the prawns into the Air Fryer tray and cook for 7 minutes
4. Whilst the prawns are cooking, mix the ketchup, cider and mayonnaise to from the sauce
5. Serve whilst crispy with cocktail sauce on the side

CRUMBED CHICKEN STRIPS

Ingredients
1 Chicken Breast, cut into strips
1/2 Tsp Balsamic Vinegar
1 Cup Breadcrumbs
1/2 Tsp Black Pepper
1 Tsp Brown Sugar
2 Tbsps Soy Sauce
2 Egg Whites
1 Tsp Flour
1 Pinch Salt

Directions
1. Add the soy sauce, sugar, flour and vinegar into a bowl and mix
2. Take the chicken strips and toss into this mixture until evenly coated. Allow to marinate for an hour
3. Preheat the Air Fryer to 350 degrees
4. Using separate bowls, dip the marinated chicken strips into the egg white. Next dip into the breadcrumbs so they are well covered
5. Place strips into the Air Fryer tray for 12 minutes then turn them over for a further 10 minutes until crispy
6. Serve with preferred sauce

DUTCH CROQUETTES

Ingredients
1 lb Minced Veal
1 Tsp Worcestershire Sauce
1 ½ Cups Seasoned Breadcrumbs
2 Tbsps Butter
1 Cup Flour
1/2 Cup Milk
1/2 Cup Chicken Broth
1/2 Tsp Paprika
1/2 Tsp Salt
1/4 Tsp Pepper
1 Tsp Parsley, chopped
2 Tbsps Water
1 Egg

Directions
1. In a pan, cook the veal over a medium flame until brown
2. In another pan over low heat, add the butter and half a cup of the flour, stirring until there are no lumps. Slowly add the chicken broth and milk to form a thickened sauce. Combine with the browned veal and add the salt and pepper, paprika, parsley and Worcestershire. Cook for a further minute and then allow to cool
3. Taking a large spoonful of the veal mixture, shape into thumb sized cylinders. Ensure that you tightly pack the mix to hold firm
4. Put the breadcrumbs in a shallow bowl. Then mix the water and egg in another bowl. Cover the croquettes with the flour, then coat in the egg mix, and finally cover with the breadcrumbs. Do this twice for a crispier coating
5. Preheat the Air Fryer to 350 degrees
6. Fry croquettes for 6 minutes until lightly brown and serve whilst crispy

FALAFEL WITH CUCUMBER SAUCE

Ingredients
For the Falafel:
15 Oz Can Chickpeas, drained
1 Onion, chopped
1/2 Cup Parsley
2 Cloves Garlic, minced
1 Cup Breadcrumbs
2 Tsps Ground Cumin
1 Tsp Ground Coriander
1 Tsp Salt
1 Pinch Cayenne Pepper
1 Tsp Lemon Juice
1 Tsp Baking Powder
1 Tbsp Oil
1 Egg

For the Sauce:
6 Ozs Plain Yogurt
1/2 Cucumber, peeled and mashed
1 Tsp Dried Dill Weed
Salt and Pepper to taste
1 Tbsp Mayonnaise

Directions
1. To make the sauce, combine all listed ingredients in a bowl. Place into the refrigerator for at least 20 minutes
2. To form the falafels, combine the parsley, garlic and onion in a food processor until it is a smooth consistency. Add the chickpeas and mash until it forms a thick paste
3. Place the oil, egg, cumin, coriander, cayenne pepper, lemon juice, baking powder and salt, pepper into a bowl. Combine this with the chickpea mixture whilst gradually adding the breadcrumbs
4. Take heaped spoonfuls of the mixture and form into small balls

5. Preheat Air Fryer at 350 degrees
6. Cook the falafels in the Air Fryer for 8 minutes until brown and crispy
7. Serve with chilled cucumber sauce

FETA TRIANGLES

Ingredients
3 Ozs Feta Cheese
2 Tbsps Parsley, diced
4 Sheets Puff Pastry
Cooking Spray
1 Egg Yolk
Pepper to season

Directions
1. In a small bowl, whisk together the cheese, pepper, yolk and parsley
2. Slice each pastry sheet into 3 even strips. Place a spoonful of the cheese mix on the center of each pastry strip, then fold the remaining ends together and secure to form a triangle
3. Heat the Air Fryer to 375 degrees
4. Lightly cover the triangles with some cooking spray and place into the Air Fryer. Cook for 2 to 3 minutes until crispy
5. Serve with sweet chili sauce

FILIPINO FRIED CHICKEN

Ingredients
2.2 lbs Chicken Wings
6 Garlic Cloves, minced
2 Bay Leaves
1 Tsp Black Peppercorns, crushed
3/4 Cup Soy Sauce
1 Cup White Vinegar
1 ½ Cups Water

Directions
1. In a large pan, combine the chicken, garlic, peppercorns, bay leaves, soy sauce, vinegar and water and bring to a boil. Simmer uncovered over low heat until chicken is cooked through for about 30 minutes
2. Remove chicken from pan and pat dry
3. Heat the Air Fryer to 350 degrees
4. Place the chicken into the Air Fryer tray and cook for another 5 to 7 minutes until crispy
5. Serve hot with rice

FISH SANDWICHES

Ingredients
2 lbs White Fish Fillets
1/4 Cup Yellow Cornmeal
1 Tsp Greek Seasoning
Salt and Pepper to taste
2 ½ Cups Plain Flour
2 Tsps Baking Powder
2 Cups Beer
4 Hamburger Buns
Mayonnaise
Lettuce Leaves
1 Tomato, sliced
1 Egg

Directions
1. Cut the fish fillets into burger patty sized strips. Season with salt and pepper to desired taste
2. In a medium bowl, mix together the beer, egg, baking powder, plain flour, cornmeal, Greek seasoning and additional salt and pepper
3. Heat the Air Fryer to 340 degrees
4. Place each seasoned fish strip into the batter, ensuring that it is well coated
5. Place battered fish into the Air Fryer tray and cook in batches for 6 minutes or until crispy
6. Compile the sandwich by topping each bun with mayonnaise, then a lettuce leaf, tomato slices, and finally the cooked fish strip

FLAVOURSOME MEATBALLS

Ingredients
1 lb Ground Beef
1/2 Tsp Salt
1 Onion, diced
1/2 Tsp Garlic Salt
1 ½ Tsps Italian Seasoning
3/4 Tsp Dried Oregano
3/4 Tsp Red Pepper Powder
2 Tsps Hot Sauce
1 ½ Tbsps Worcestershire Sauce
1/3 Cup Milk
1/4 Cup Parmesan Cheese, grated
1/2 Cup Panko Breadcrumbs

Directions
1. Preheat the Air Fryer at 390 degrees
2. In a large bowl, combine the meat, diced onion, salt and garlic salt, Italian seasoning, oregano, red pepper powder, hot sauce and Worcestershire. Mix well until an even consistency is reached
3. Pour in the milk, panko and cheese, combining thoroughly
4. Take small handfuls of the mixture and roll into small meatballs. Ensure that they hold firm
5. Place in the Air Fryer tray and fry for 15 to 20 minutes until they are cooked through

FRIED BEEF ROLLS

Ingredients
11 Ozs Beef Mince
30 Spring Roll Wrappers
4 Eggs
4 Scallions, diced
2 Tsps Salt
2 Tsps Ground Coriander

Directions
1. Preheat the Air Fryer to 390 degrees
2. Brown the beef in a pan over medium to high heat. Pour out excess liquid and allow to cool
3. Combine the beef with coriander, salt, 3 eggs and scallions
4. Whisk the remaining egg in a separate bowl
5. Lay down each wrapper on a clean surface and fill with a large spoonful of the beef filling. Roll to form a cylinder shape and fold in the edges to secure, using the egg to seal the wrapper at the ends
6. Place rolls into the Air Fryer tray and cook for 10 to 12 minutes until crispy
7. Serve with sweet chili sauce

FRIED CALAMARI

Ingredients
1 ½ lbs Squid
1 ½ Cups Milk
1 Cup All Purpose Flour
1 Tsp Paprika
1 Tsp Garlic Powder
1/4 Tsp Black Pepper
1/2 Tsp Salt

Directions
1. Rinse squid well in cold water. Cut the tentacles and hood off into bite sized pieces. Ensure each piece is roughly the same size. Soak the pieces in the milk for at least 5 minutes
2. Combine the flour, paprika, garlic powder, salt, and black pepper in a bowl
3. Remove the squid from the milk and coat each piece in the flour mixture
4. Heat the Air Fryer to 390 degrees and add battered pieces into the tray in batches. Cook for 10 minutes or until the calamari is crispy
5. Serve with tartare sauce or with lemon wedges

FRIED CRAB STICKS

Ingredients
12 Crabsticks
2 Tsps Sesame Oil
2 Tsps Cajun Seasoning

Directions
1. Preheat the Air Fryer to 320 degrees
2. Break the crab sticks length-wise and cut into even halves
3. Place pieces in a bowl and drizzle the sesame oil over until well combined
4. Put crab sticks into the Air Fryer tray for 12 minutes until golden brown. Shake the tray after 5 minutes to ensure that crab sticks are cooked evenly
5. Remove and season with Cajun seasoning to taste

FRIED GREEN SPANISH OLIVES

Ingredient
14 Ozs Spanish Stuffed Olives, drained
1/3 Cup Flour
2 Eggs, beaten
1 Tbsp Milk
1 ½ Cups Breadcrumbs
1 ½ Cups Grated Parmesan Cheese
Pinch of Cayenne Pepper

Directions
1. Place the flour on a plate. Combine the egg and milk in a bowl. Combine the breadcrumbs, parmesan and cayenne pepper in a bowl
2. Dip olives in flour and shake off excess. Dip in the egg mixture, then in the breadcrumb mixture, pressing to coat. Place in the fridge for 15 minutes to chill
3. Preheat the Air Fryer to 350 degrees
4. Cook battered olives in batches in the Air Fryer for 2 to 3 minutes or until crispy
5. Place in a serving bowl and serve

FRIED GRILLED CHEESE SANDWICH BITES

Ingredients
8 Slices Bread
8 Slices American Cheese
1/2 Cup Mayonnaise
2 Eggs, whisked
2/3 Cup Milk
1 ½ Sleeves Ritz Crackers, crumbed

Directions
1. Lay out the bread and spread mayonnaise onto one side of each slice. Add 1-2 slices of cheese to 4 slices of the bread. Place the lid on, with mayonnaise side down
2. Cut each sandwich in quarters
3. In separate bowl, whisk together the eggs and milk. In another dish add the breadcrumbs
4. Dredge each sandwich quarter in the egg and then the crackers. Place in the fridge to rest for one hour
5. Heat the Air Fryer to 340 degrees
6. Cook sandwich quarters in batches for about 4 minutes until golden and the cheese is melted
7. Serve whilst crispy

FRIED OYSTERS

Ingredients
6 Oysters, rinsed and drained
1 Egg, beaten
1 ½ Cups Panko Breadcrumbs
1 Cup Ketchup
1 Tbsp Horseradish
1/4 Tsp Chili Sauce

Directions
1. Dip the oysters in the egg, and then coat in the Panko
2. Combine the chili sauce, ketchup and horseradish. Allow to chill in the refrigerator
3. Heat the Air Fryer to 320 degrees
4. Place crumbed oysters into the Air Fryer tray and cook for 4 minutes until the crumbs are crispy
5. Serve hot with the sauce mixture

FRIED PEANUT BUTTER AND JELLY SANDWICHES

Ingredients
2 Tbsps Sugar
1 ½ Tbsps Ground Cinnamon
4 Tbsps Unsalted Butter
8 Slices Bread
6 Tbsps Fruit Jam
6 Tbsps Peanut Butter

Directions
1. In a small bowl, combine the sugar and cinnamon
2. Spread the butter on one side of each bread slice. Flip the remaining slices over and spread them with the jam. Flip the remaining slices over and spread them with the peanut butter. Sandwich together the jam slices and the peanut butter slices, keeping the buttered sides of the bread facing outwards
3. Heat the Air Fryer to 340 degrees
4. Sprinkle the cinnamon sugar over the top of each sandwich and place into the Air Fryer. Cook for 2 to 3 minutes
5. Flip the sandwiches over and sprinkle the tops with cinnamon sugar. Continue to cook for 2 to 3 minutes
6. Remove the sandwiches and cut into quarters to serve

FRIED PICKLES

Ingredients
16 Oz Jar Dill Pickle Spears
1/4 Cup Milk
1/2 Cup White Flour
1/2 Tsp Salt
1/2 Tsp Garlic Powder
1/2 Tsp Paprika

Directions
1. Remove pickles from jar and blot with a paper towel until they are dry
2. Whisk the milk and egg in a bowl
3. In a separate bowl, combine all dry ingredients
4. Dip the pickle wedges into the dry mix, then into the egg mix, then back in the flour mix for additional coating
5. Place battered pickles into the Air Fryer for 10 minutes at 390 degrees until golden brown
6. Serve with preferred hot sauce

FRIED RAVIOLI

Ingredients
1 Pack Frozen Ravioli
1 Tbsp Olive Oil
2 Tbsps Parmesan Cheese
2 Tsps Garlic Powder

Directions
1. Place frozen ravioli into the Air Fryer tray and drizzle with olive oil
2. Cook at 350 degrees for approximately 13 minutes or until the ends of the ravioli are brown and crisp
3. Shake the tray after 7 minutes to ensure that all pieces are cooked evenly
4. Once cooked, sprinkle with parmesan cheese and garlic powder to serve

HERB AND GARLIC FISH FINGERS

Ingredients
14 Ozs White Fish Fillets, cut into strips
2 Tbsps Lemon Juice
1/2 Tsp Turmeric
1/2 Tsp Chili flakes
2 Tsps Mixed Dried Herbs
2 Tsps Garlic Powder
1/2 Tsp Black Pepper
1/2 Tsp Salt
2 Tbsps Maida Flour
1 Tsp Rice Flour
2 Tsps Cornflour
2 Eggs
1/4 Tsp Baking Soda
1 Cup Breadcrumbs

Directions
1. Place fish strips into a bowl and add salt, lemon juice, turmeric powder, red chili flakes, black pepper, one teaspoon of the mixed herbs, and one teaspoon of the garlic. Mix well and marinate for 15 minutes
2. Combine maida, rice flour, cornflour, egg and baking soda in another bowl
3. Add the marinated fish strips to this mixture
4. Mix the remaining teaspoon of mixed herbs and garlic in the breadcrumbs. Coat the fish fingers evenly with this mixture
5. Preheat the Air Fryer to 350 degrees. Place strips into tray and fry for 10 minutes until crispy and browned
6. Serve with ketchup or tartare sauce

HOMEMADE NACHOS

Ingredients
1/2 Cup Sweet Corn
1 Cup All Purpose Flour
1/2 Tsp Chili Powder
1 Tbsp Butter
1/4 Cup Water
1 Tsp Salt

Directions
1. Combine the water with the sweet corn and grind to a fine paste
2. In a bowl, add the flour, salt, chili powder and butter and combine the ingredients well. Mix in with the sweet corn paste until it forms a dough
3. Preheat the Air Fryer at 350 degrees
4. On a clean surface, sprinkle some flour and roll the dough into a thin sheet. Cut out nachos into small triangles or desired shape
5. Place the nachos in the Air Fryer tray and cook for 6 minutes or until crispy and brown
6. Serve with salsa or topped with cheese

INDIAN NAVAJO FRY BREAD

Ingredients
2 ½ Cups Flour
1 Tsp Baking Powder
1 Tsp Sugar
1 Tsp Oil
1 Cup Warm Milk
1 Tsp Salt
2 Tsps Yeast

Directions
1. Preheat the Air Fryer to 390 degrees
2. In a large mixing bowl pour the warm milk then add all dry ingredients and oil. Combine until the mixture forms a dough. Cover for 20 minutes and allow to rise
3. Once the dough has risen, shape into palm sized discs
4. Place into the Air Fryer and fry for 5 to 7 minutes until golden brown
5. Serve with honey and butter as a snack

JALAPENO BITES

Ingredients
2 Jalapeno Peppers
1 Oz Cheddar Cheese
1 Spring Roll Wrapper
1 Egg, beaten

Directions
1. Chop the stem end off of the peppers and slice lengthwise, trim out inner white pith and all seeds
2. Divide the cheese into strips
3. Cut the spring roll wrapper in half and brush each side with the beaten egg
4. Place a half of jalapeno in one corner of the spring roll wrapper half and place a strip of cheese in the cavity, and top with the other half of that jalapeno pepper
5. Holding the two halves of the pepper together, roll the pepper up tightly in the spring roll wrapper on the diagonal, folding the edges in.
Glue down any loose wrapping with a brush of the egg
6. Preheat the Air Fryer to 350 degrees
7. Place jalapeno bites into the tray and cook for 10 minutes until light brown
8. Serve piping hot with aioli

JERK CHICKEN WINGS

Ingredients
4 lbs Chicken Wings
2 Tbsps Olive Oil
2 Tbsps Soy Sauce
1 Tbsp Minced Garlic
1 Habanero Pepper, seeded and chopped
1 Tbsp Allspice
1 Tsp Cinnamon
1 Tsp Cayenne Pepper
1 Tsp White Pepper
1 Tsp Salt
2 Tbsps Sugar
1 Tbsp Thyme, finely chopped
1 Tbsp Grated Ginger
4 Scallions, chopped
5 Tbsps Lime Juice
1/2 Cup Red Wine Vinegar

Directions
1. Combine all ingredients in a mixing bowl, covering the chicken thoroughly with the seasonings and marinade
2. Transfer to a large zip lock bag and refrigerate for a minimum of 2 hours or overnight
3. Preheat the Air Fryer to 390 degrees
4. Remove the wings from the bag and drain all liquid
5. Place half the wings in the Air Fryer and cook each batch for 18 to 20 minutes, shaking halfway through
6. Serve with blue cheese dipping sauce

KALE CHIPS

Ingredients
1 Bunch Kale
2 Tbsps Olive Oil
Sea Salt

Directions
1. Wash and thoroughly dry the kale in a salad spinner
2. Remove the ribs from the kale and cut into 1 1/2-inch pieces
3. Toss with the olive oil and salt until evenly coated
4. Place in the Air Fryer at 390 degrees for 2 to 3 minutes, tossing the leaves halfway through

LASAGNA CUPCAKES

Ingredients
12 Ozs Minced Beef
Salt and Pepper to taste
1 ½ Cups Parmesan Cheese
1 ½ Cups Mozzarella Cheese
3/4 Cup Ricotta Cheese
1 Cup Tomato Based Pasta Sauce
20 Round Wonton Wrappers
1 Tbsp Basil
* Silicon Muffin Cups

Directions
1. Heat the Air Fryer to 390 degrees
2. In a saucepan, brown the beef and season to taste with salt and pepper
3. Set aside half a cup each of the Mozzarella and Parmesan to use on top of the lasagna
4. To layer the cupcakes, place a wrapper at the bottom of the muffin cup. Then place equal amounts of each of the cheeses in, a spoonful of the beef, and finally the pasta sauce. Finish with reserved cheeses
5. Place cupcakes into the Air Fryer and bake for 15 minutes or more until the upper cheese layer is crispy
6. Sprinkle with basil to serve

LEMON FRIED CHORIZO

Ingredients
3 Chorizo Sausages
2 Tbsps Honey
1 Tbsp Lemon Juice
1 Tbsp Chopped Parsley

Directions
1. Slice each chorizo into even pieces
2. Combine all ingredients into a bowl and allow chorizo slices to marinate for 20 minutes
3. Preheat the Air Fryer to 350 degrees
4. Place chorizo into the Air Fryer tray and cook for 5 minutes until crispy and honey has caramelized
5. Serve with lemon wedges

LEMONED TUNA PATTIES

Ingredients
12 Ozs Canned Tuna
2 Tsps Dijon Mustard
1/2 Cup Panko Breadcrumbs
1 Tbsp Lemon Juice
2 Tbsps Chopped Parsley
3 Tbsps Olive Oil
1/2 Tsp Tabasco sauce
Salt and Pepper to taste
1 Egg

Directions
1. Drain liquid from the canned tuna. Mix the tuna, mustard, breadcrumbs, lemon juice, chopped parsley and tabasco sauce in a bowl
2. Season the mixture with salt and pepper, then add the egg and combine
3. Place a sheet of baking paper onto a plate, then spoon the tuna mixture into patties. Refrigerate for an hour or overnight if possible. This will help retain the shape of the patties
4. Once the patties are ready, place them in the Air Fryer and set to 350 degrees for 12 minutes
5. Serve cooked patties with a drizzle of lemon juice and tartare sauce

MACARONI AND CHEESE ROUNDS

Ingredients
1/2 lb Rotelle Pasta
1/2 Cup Milk
1/2 Cup Heavy Cream
1/2 Cup Grated Fontina Cheese
1/2 Cup Grated Gruyere Cheese
1/2 Cup Grated Sharp Cheddar Cheese
1/4 Tsp Cayenne Pepper
1/8 Tsp Nutmeg
1/4 Cup Breadcrumbs
1 Tbsp Melted Butter
1 Tbsp Salt
* Small Round Baking Tray

Directions
1. Cook the pasta according to packet instructions until just al dente and then drain
2. In the round baking tray, add the pasta, milk, heavy cream, cheeses, cayenne pepper and nutmeg and stir well to combine
3. Combine the breadcrumbs and melted butter in a separate bowl
4. Sprinkle over the top of the pasta and place round tray into the Air Fryer. Set the temperature to 350 degrees for 30 minutes
5. Once cooked through, allow to cool for at least 20 minutes before inverting the round tray over a plate and tapping to remove the macaroni and cheese wheel
6. Cut into wedges and serve warm

MEATBALLS IN TOMATO SAUCE

Ingredients
11 Ozs Ground Beef
1 Cup Tomato Based Pasta Sauce
1 Tbsp Parsley, chopped
1/2 Tbsp Thyme, chopped
3 Tbsps Breadcrumbs
Salt and Pepper to taste
1 Onion, chopped
1 Egg
* Small Oven Dish

Directions
1. Place all the ingredients into a bowl and mix well. Shape the mixture into 10 to 12 balls
2. Preheat the Air Fryer to 390 degrees
3. Place the meatballs in the Air Fryer and cook for 7 minutes
4. Transfer the meatballs to an oven dish, add the tomato sauce and place the dish into the Air Fryer. Reduce the temperature to 320 degrees and cook for another 5 minutes to sauté the sauce through
5. Transfer onto a plate to serve

MEDITERRANEAN CHICKEN BITES

Ingredients
10 Ozs Minced Chicken
1 Cup Breadcrumbs
1 Tbsp Hot Paprika
1 Egg Yolk and 2 Egg Whites
2 Cloves Garlic, minced
1 ½ Tbsps Red Pesto
Salt and Pepper to taste
1 Tbsp Olive Oil

Directions
1. In a bowl, mix the paprika, oil and breadcrumbs together
2. In another bowl, combine the chicken, minced garlic, red presto, yolk, and salt and pepper
3. Heat the Air Fryer to 390 degrees
4. Beat the egg whites and place in a shallow bowl
5. Take spoonfuls of the chicken mix and shape into 12 small round bites
6. Dip each bite in the egg white, then into the crumb mixture
7. Place bites in the Air Fryer tray for 12 minutes until golden brown. This may need to be done in batches. Repeat process until all pieces are cooked
8. Serve with tomato sauce

MOROCCAN MEATBALLS WITH MINT DIP

Ingredients
For the Meatballs:
1 lb Ground Lamb
4 Ozs Turkey Mince
1 Tbsp Parsley, finely chopped
1 Tbsp Mint, finely chopped
1 Tsp Ground Cumin
1 Tsp Ground Coriander
1 Tsp Cayenne Pepper
1 Tsp Red Chili Powder
4 Minced Garlic Cloves
1/4 Cup Olive Oil
1 Tsp Salt
1 Egg White

For the Mint Dip:
1/2 Cup Greek Yogurt
1/4 Cup Sour Cream
2 Tbsps Buttermilk
1/4 Cup Mint, finely chopped

Directions
1. Preheat the Air Fryer to 390 degrees
2. In a large mixing bowl, combine all ingredients for the meatballs. Roll the meatballs into small golf ball sized pieces
3. Place half the meatballs into the Air Fryer and cook each batch for 6 to 8 minutes
4. While the meatballs are cooking, add all of the ingredients for the mint dip to a bowl and combine well
5. Serve dip with the meatballs whilst hot

MOZZARELLA CHEESE STICKS

Ingredients
10 Oz Block of Mozzarella Cheese
1 Egg
1 Tsp Garlic Powder
1/2 Tsp Salt
1 Cup Panko Breadcrumbs
Cooking Spray

Directions:
1. Cut the mozzarella into strips
2. Whisk the egg with garlic powder and salt
3. Dip each strip into the egg mixture then dredge them into the breadcrumbs until well coated. Repeat this process twice for additional crispiness
4. Freeze the battered strips for 20 to 30 minutes to set. Once set, remove from the freezer and spray with oil until each strip is lightly coated
5. Air fry the strips at 390 degrees for 5 minutes, checking for brownness at the mid-point
6. Serve hot with a spicy dip

NACHO PRAWNS

Ingredients
9 Ozs Nacho Corn Chips
18 Prawns
1 Egg

Directions
1. Prepare the prawns by removing the veins and shells, apart from the last bit of the tails. Clean, wash and pat dry
2. Place the eggs in a bowl and whisk. Crush the nacho chips in another bowl until the crumbs are finely minced
3. Dip each prawn in the whisked egg then in the chip crumbs
4. Preheat the Air Fryer to 350 degrees
5. Place the crumbed prawns in the Air Fryer tray and cook for 8 minutes
6. Serve with traditional nachos toppings such as sour cream, guacamole and salsa

POT STICKERS

Ingredients
1/2 Tsps Garlic, finely chopped
1/2 Tsp White Pepper Powder
1 Tbsp Spring Onion, finely chopped
2 Cups All Purpose Flour
1 Cup Cabbage, grated
4 Green Chilies
1/2 Cup Sweet Corn
1/4 Cup Hot Water
1/2 Tsp Soy Sauce
1 Tsp Sesame Seeds
1 Tbsp Butter
1 Tsp Salt

Directions
1. For the stuffing, combine the cabbage, finely garlic, sweet corn, spring onion, green chili, pepper powder, soy sauce, sesame seeds and butter
2. Take a bowl and add flour, salt and hot water to form a dough. Knead well and set aside
3. On a clean surface, sprinkle some flour and roll the dough into a thin sheet. Using the top of a cup head, cut out small circular pot stickers
4. Spoon the stuffing into the pot stickers and apply water to the edges to seal into a dumpling shape
5. Preheat the Air Fryer at 350 degrees
6. Place the pot stickers in the Air Fryer to fry for 13 minutes until crispy
7. Serve with preferred sauce

POTATO AND ARUGULA CROQUETTES

Ingredients
2 Potatoes
1/2 Cup Arugula, steamed
1/2 Cup Feta Cheese, crumbled
2 Garlic Cloves, minced
1 Pinch Red Pepper Flakes
Salt and Pepper to taste
1 Egg
2 Eggs, slightly beaten
1/8 Cup Cream
1/2 Cup Flour
1/2 Cup Breadcrumbs

Directions
1. Peel and quarter the potatoes, then boil them in salted water. Mash well once they are cooked
2. Combine the arugula, feta, garlic, red pepper flakes and one egg together and blend thoroughly
3. Take spoonful's of the mixture and roll to form small cylinders or croquettes
4. Place the flour in one bowl. Beat 2 eggs with cream and place in a second bowl. Finally, arrange the breadcrumbs in a third bowl
5. Dip each croquette in the flour then egg and then roll in the crumbs
6. Preheat the Air Fryer to 350 degrees
7. Cook the croquettes in the Air Fryer for 6 minutes or until golden and crispy
8. Season with salt and pepper to serve

POTATO CROQUETTES

Ingredients
2 Russet Potatoes
1 Egg Yolk
1/2 Cup Parmesan Cheese
2 Tbsps Flour
2 Tbsps Chives, finely chopped
Salt and Black Pepper to taste
1 Pinch Nutmeg

For the Filling:
2 Tbsps Olive Oil
1 Cup Flour
2 Eggs, beaten
1/2 Cup Breadcrumbs

Directions
1. Peel the potatoes and boil them in a pot until softened. Mash whilst still hot and then set aside to cool
2. Once cooled, mix the mashed potato with the Parmesan, flour, yolk nutmeg, salt and pepper and chives
3. Take spoonfuls of the mixture and shape into small cylinders
4. Heat the Air Fryer to 390 degrees
5. Combine the olive oil and crumbs in a shallow bowl
6. Gently roll the balls in flour, then coat with the eggs, and finally into the crumb mix
7. Place the croquettes into the Air Fryer and cook for 6 minutes until the coating has browned
8. Serve with ranch or tomato based sauce

PORK FRIES

Ingredients
1.3 lb Pork Tenderloin
8 Ozs Panko Breadcrumbs
1 Tbsp Brown Sugar
1 Tsp Cumin
2/3 Cup Flour
4 Eggs

Directions
1. Using a sharp knife, cut the pork lengthwise into even strips, the size of chips or fries
2. Whisk the eggs and place them in a bowl. Mix the sugar, cumin and flour together in another bowl. Finally, pour the breadcrumbs onto a plate
3. Preheat the Air Fryer to 390 degrees
4. Place the pork fries into the Air Fryer, ensuring that they do not overlap
5. Fry for 6 minutes until golden brown and the pork is tender
6. Serve hot with preferred sauce

PRAWN AND PORK NOODLE BALLS

Ingredients
11 Ozs Prawns
14 Ozs Ground Pork
2 Shallots, diced
1 Tbsp Oyster Sauce
1/4 Tsp Sesame Oil
7 Ozs Pre-Fried Noodles
1 Baby Cos Lettuce
Sweet Chili Sauce

Directions
1. Wash, peel and devein the prawns
2. Use a rolling pin to crush the pre fried noodles until they form loose crumbs
3. In a food processor, combine the peeled prawns, pork, oyster sauce, shallots and sesame oil
4. Roll spoonfuls of the prawn mixture into balls, then roll the balls onto the noodles
5. Preheat the Air Fryer to 350 degrees
6. Add the balls into the Air Fryer tray and cook for 4 to 5 minutes or until cooked through. Repeat more batches if necessary
7. Arrange baby cos leaves on a platter. Place 2 to 3 prawn balls in each leaf and serve with sweet chili sauce

PROSCUITTO AND SPINACH ARANCINI

Ingredients
4 Slices Prosciutto, diced
8 Ozs Grated Parmesan Cheese
3 Ozs Mozzarella Cheese, sliced
2 Ozs Baby Spinach, diced
2 Cups Breadcrumbs
3 Garlic Cloves, minced
1 ½ Cups Risotto Rice
1 Liter Chicken Stock
2 Tsps Olive Oil
1 Onion, diced
2/3 Cup Flour
3 Eggs

Directions
1. In a pan, heat the oil and cook the onion and garlic until soft. When fragrant, add the prosciutto and cook for the further minute
2. Place rice and stock into the pan and simmer until the liquid is completely reduced. Throw Parmesan and spinach into the mix and remove from heat. Allow the mixture to cool in the refrigerator for at least an hour
3. Whisk the eggs in the bowl, then place the flour on a plate, and finally the breadcrumbs on another plate
4. Take large spoonfuls of the risotto mix and roll into balls. Push a small hole into the middle of each ball and then fill with some Mozzarella
5. Coat each ball in the flour, then in the egg, and then into the breadcrumbs
6. Heat the Air Fryer to 375 degrees
7. Place the arancini balls into the Air Fryer and cook in batches 5 minutes or until golden

REUBEN EGG ROLLS

Ingredients
5 Ozs Corned Beef
5 Slices Gruyere Cheese
1 ½ Cups Sauerkraut
10 Egg Roll Wrappers
1 Egg, beaten
Mayonnaise to serve

Directions
1. Cut the corned beef and cheese into thin strips
2. Preheat the Air Fryer at 390 degrees
3. Place wrappers onto a clean surface and brush the edges with egg
4. Position 2 strips each of the cheese and corned beef in the middle of each wrapper. Finish with a spoon of sauerkraut
5. Fold the two sides of the wrapper towards the center to enclose the filling. Then roll the wrapper into a cylinder shape and secure the end to enclose the egg roll
6. Place the egg rolls into the Air Fryer tray in batches. Allow to cook for 5 minutes until all sides are golden brown
7. Serve hot with the mayonnaise

RISOTTO BALLS

Ingredients
4 Ozs Risotto Rice
2 Tbsps Olive Oil
1 Shallot, finely chopped
4 Ozs Mushrooms, chopped
1 Cup Chicken Stock
1 Tbsp Grated Parmesan Cheese
Salt and Pepper to taste
1 Cup Breadcrumbs
1 Egg, beaten

Directions
1. Heat up olive oil in a pan and sauté the shallot. Add the mushrooms and fry until the liquid has almost evaporated
2. Stir in the rice grains and fry until shiny. Add the stock and slow boil the rice for 20 minutes
3. Mix the cheese through the risotto and season to taste with salt and pepper
4. Allow the risotto to cool down and refrigerate for at least one hour
5. Shape the risotto into walnut-sized balls. Coat the balls in the beaten egg and then in the breadcrumbs
6. Place balls into the Air Fryer for 7 minutes at 390 degrees, they should be golden brown when ready
7. Serve with tomato based sauce or pesto

ROSEMARY RUSSET POTATO CHIPS

Ingredients
2 Medium Russet Potatoes
1/4 Cup Olive Oil
1/2 Cup Sour Cream
2 Tsp Chopped Rosemary
1 Tbsp Roasted Garlic
1 Pinch Salt

Directions
1. Preheat the Air Fryer to 390 degrees
2. Take one head of garlic, cut the topside off. Placed into aluminum foil with one tablespoon of olive oil, salt, and cook in the Air Fryer for 20 minutes. When finished cool and set aside
3. Scrub potatoes under running water and cut lengthwise. Using a peeler, peel potato strips into a bowl full of water
4. Soak potatoes for 30 minutes, changing the water several times to remove starch
5. Preheat the Air Fryer to 320 degrees
6. In a mixing bowl, toss potato strips with remaining olive oil
7. Place chips into the Air Fryer and cook for 20 minutes until golden brown
8. While the chips are cooking, combine sour cream, roasted garlic, 1/2 tablespoon chopped rosemary and salt to form a dip
9. Finish the potato chips with remaining chopped rosemary and salt

SALMON CROQUETTES

Ingredients
15 Oz Tin of Red Salmon, drained
2 Eggs, beaten
1/2 Cup Parsley, chopped
1/2 Tsp Cayenne Pepper
1/2 Tsp Garlic Powder
1/2 Cup Breadcrumbs
1 Tbsp Olive Oil

Directions
1. Preheat the Air Fryer to 390 degrees
2. With a fork, mash up the salmon and mix with the egg, herbs, and seasoning
3. In a separate bowl, combine the breadcrumbs and oil
4. Shape the salmon mix into 16 small croquettes and coat them in the crumb mixture
5. In batches, put the croquettes in the tray and slide into the Air Fryer for 7 minutes until crispy
6. Serve with a side salad or creamy dip

SALT AND PEPPER CHICKEN WINGS

Ingredients
30 Chicken Wings
3 Tsps Salt
4 Tsps Black Pepper
4 Tsps Sesame Oil
5 Cloves Garlic, minced
4 Green Onions, chopped

Directions
1. Preheat the Air Fryer at 390 degrees
2. Season the chicken with salt and pepper, ensuring that you coat evenly
3. Place the wings into the Air Fryer tray and cook for 12 minutes. Shake the tray and then resume cooking for another 12 minutes. Remove and place on a serving platter
4. Using a pan, heat the sesame oil and then cook the green onions and garlic until they soften
5. Pour the hot oil mix over the wings, ensuring that each piece is covered
6. Serve whilst crispy

SAUERKRAUT BALLS

Ingredients
8 Ozs Sausage, crumbled
1/4 Cup Onion, finely chopped
1 Can Sauerkraut, drained and sliced
3 Ozs Cream Cheese
2 Tsps Parsley
1 Tsp Mustard
Garlic Salt
1/4 Tsp Black Pepper
1/4 Cup Flour
2 Eggs, beaten
1/4 Cup Milk
1 Cup Breadcrumbs

Directions
1. In a saucepan, cook the sausage and onion until the meat has browned. Allow to cool
2. Pour meat into a bowl and add sauerkraut, cream cheese, parsley, mustard, garlic salt and pepper. Chill the mixture for one hour
3. Combine the eggs and milk into a bowl and set aside
4. Taking spoonful's of the mixture, form into small balls and coat with flour
5. Dip the balls in the egg-milk mixture and then roll into the breadcrumbs
6. Preheat the Air Fryer to 390 degrees
7. Place balls into the Air Fryer and cook for 15 to 18 minutes. Serve hot

SAUSAGE AND SAGE STUFFING BALLS

Ingredients
3 ½ Ozs Sausage Meat
1/2 Diced Onion
1/2 Tsp Minced Garlic
1 Tsp Sage
3 Tbsp Breadcrumbs
Salt and Pepper to taste

Directions
1. Place all ingredients into a bowl and mix until there is uniform consistency
2. Roll into medium sized balls and place them in the Air Fryer tray
3. Cook at 350 degrees for 15 minutes and then serve

SAUSAGE ROLLS

Ingredients
12 Ozs Cocktail Franks
2 Sheets Puff Pastry

Directions
1. Remove the cocktail franks from the package and drain, then pat dry on paper towels
2. Cut the puff pastry into rectangular strips, approximately 1-inch x 1.5-inch. Roll the strips around the franks, leaving the ends visible. Place in the freezer for 5 minutes to firm
3. Preheat the Air Fryer to 320 degrees
4. Remove the franks from the freezer and place half of them in the Air Fryer tray
5. Cook each batch for 6 to 8 minutes or until golden brown

SEAFOOD SKEWERS WITH LIME MAYONNAISE

Ingredients
11 Ozs Firm White Fish Fillets
8 Crab Sticks, halved
8 Jumbo Shrimps
Salt and Pepper to taste
1 Lime, zested and juiced
1/2 Cup Mayonnaise
1 Tbsp Roasted Sesame Seeds
* Wooden Skewers

Directions
1. Preheat the Air Fryer at 350 degrees
2. Mix the mayonnaise with 2 tablespoons of lime juice, zest, and season with salt and pepper
3. Dice the fish into 16 cubes. Assemble onto wooden skewers by alternating 2 cubes of white fish, 2 pieces of crab stick and finishing with shrimp
4. Place skewers into the Air Fryer for 5 to 7 minutes until seafood is cooked through
5. Sprinkle the seafood skewers with sesame seeds and serve with lime mayonnaise

SESAME PRAWN TOASTS

Ingredients
8 King Prawns
3 Ozs Smoked Trout
1 Onion, chopped
4 Slices of Bread
3 Tbsps Sesame Seeds
Salt and Pepper to season

Directions
1. Clean, peel and devein each prawn
2. Combine the salt and pepper, king prawns, trout and onion in a food processor. Pulse until all ingredients are minced together
3. Remove the crusts from the bread and cut each slice in half
4. Cover each bread halve with the prawn mixture and then sprinkle sesame seeds to top
5. Preheat the Air Fryer to 350 degrees
6. Place the toasts into the Air Fryer tray and cook for two minutes until golden
7. Serve whilst hot

SLOPPY JOE'S

Ingredients
1 lb Ground Turkey
1 Tbsp Worcestershire Sauce
16 Ozs Canned Tomatoes
1 Tsp Vegetable Oil
3 Cloves Garlic
1/4 Cup Ketchup
1 Tbsp Chili Flakes
4 Hamburger Buns
1 Onion

Directions
1. Preheat the Air Fryer to 350 degrees
2. Finely dice the garlic and onion, then add to the Air Fryer tray and cook for 8 minutes with the oil
3. Add the turkey to the Air Fryer and cook for a further 5 minutes until browned
4. Using a spatula, separate the meat until it is crumbled and well combined with the garlic and onion
5. Pour the tomatoes, ketchup, Worcestershire sauce, tomato sauce and chili flakes into the tray and mix into the turkey. Cook the sloppy joe's for 15 minutes whilst stirring half way through
6. Serve on toasted hamburger buns

SOFT SHELL CRAB

Ingredients
4 Soft Shell Crabs
1/2 Cup Milk
1 Cup Flour
Salt and Pepper
1 Egg

Directions
1. Thoroughly clean and prepare each crab. Cut out and discard the gills and eyes
2. Preheat the Air Fryer to 350 degrees
3. Combine the milk and egg in a bowl. Pour the flour into another bowl and season with salt and pepper
4. Take each crab and cover in the flour mix, then into the milk and egg mixture. Finally, coat the crabs a second time in the flour for additional battering
5. In batches of two, put the crabs into the Air Fryer tray. Cook for 3 to 4 minutes until crispy
6. Serve whole seasoned with some extra pepper

SOUTHERN STYLE FRIED CHICKEN

Ingredients
5 Chicken Leg Pieces, with skin
1 ½ Tsps Cayenne Pepper
3 Cups Milk
1 Tbsp Salt
1 Cup Flour
1 Egg, beaten

Directions
1. Place chicken into a bowl and immerse with milk. Cover with cling film and place in the fridge overnight
2. Once tender, place the contents of the bowl into a pan and bring then bring to a boil. Reduce to a simmer then cool the chicken for 15 minutes
3. Preheat the Air Fryer to 375 degrees
4. Combine the pepper, flour, salt in a large bowl. Place the beaten egg in a separate bowl
5. Dip each chicken piece in the flour mixture, then in the egg. Do this twice for each piece to create a thicker coating
6. Place the chicken pieces into the Air Fryer tray and cook for 15 minutes or until browned. You may need to do this in batches
7. Serve immediately

SPICY BARBEQUE DRUMSTICKS

Ingredients
4 Chicken Drumsticks
1 Clove Garlic, crushed
1/2 Tbsp Mustard
2 Tsps Brown Sugar
1 Tsp Chili Powder
Black Pepper to taste
1 Tbsp Olive Oil

Directions
1. Preheat the Air Fryer to 390 degrees
2. Mix the garlic with the mustard, brown sugar, chili powder, oil, a pinch of salt and pepper to taste
3. Rub the drumsticks completely with the mixture and leave to marinate for 20 minutes or overnight for more intense flavor
4. Put the drumsticks in Air Fryer tray and cook for 10 minutes until brown
5. Then lower the temperature to 300 degrees and roast the drumsticks for another 10 minutes until done
6. Serve with a side salad

SPICY CHEESE BALLS

Ingredients

2 Tbsp Grated Parmesan Cheese
1/4 Cup All Purpose Flour
1 Onion, finely chopped
1 Red Bell pepper, chopped
1 Tsp Minced Garlic
1/2 Tsp Red Chili Flakes
2 Green Chilies, finely chopped
1 Tbsp Coriander, finely chopped
1 Cup Breadcrumbs
3 Tsps Butter
1/2 Cup Water
Pinch of Salt
2 Eggs, beaten
1 Tbsp Oil

Directions

1. Place water in to a saucepan and bring to boil. Add butter and mix well
2. Reduce the heat and add the salt and flour and combine well. Switch off the flame
3. Slowly add the beaten egg to the flour mixture and mix well to form a soft dough
4. In that add chopped onions, bell peppers, garlic, red chili flakes, green chilies, coriander, grated cheese and combine well
5. In a separate plate, combine the breadcrumbs and oil together
6. Spoon some balls of pastry dough and drop into the bread crumb mixture. Roll each ball so that they are evenly coated
7. Preheat the Air Fryer to 350 degrees
8. Place the balls onto the Air Fryer tray and cook for 10 minutes until crispy
9. Serve with aioli or tomato sauce

SPRING ROLLS

Ingredients
For the Filling:
4 Ozs Cooked Shredded Chicken Breast
1 Celery Stalk
1 Carrot
1/2 Cup Mushrooms
1/2 Tsp Ginger, finely chopped
1 Tsp Sugar
1 Tsp Chicken Stock Powder

For the Wrapping:
1 Egg, beaten
1 Tsp Cornstarch
8 Spring Roll Wrappers
1/2 Tsp Vegetable Oil

Directions
1. Using the filling ingredients, dice all vegetables and mix with the shredded chicken in a bowl. Add the ginger, sugar and chicken stock powder and stir evenly
2. For the wrapping, combine the egg with the cornstarch and mix to create a thick paste
3. Place some filling onto each spring roll wrapper and roll it up, sealing the ends with the egg mixture
4. Preheat the Air Fryer to 390 degrees
5. Lightly brush the spring rolls with oil prior to placing in the tray. Fry in two batches, cooking each batch for 3 to4 minutes or until golden brown
6. Serve with sweet chili sauce

TAIWANESE POPCORN CHICKEN

Ingredients
3 Boneless Chicken Thighs, cut into bite sized pieces
1 Cup Thai Basil Leaves
1 Cup Cornstarch
1 Egg, whisked
1 Tbsp Five Spice Powder

For the Marinade:
2 Garlic Cloves, minced
2 Tbsp Soy Sauce
1 Tbsp Five Spice Powder
1/2 Tsp Sesame Oil
1/2 Tbsp Shaoxing Cooking Wine
1/2 Tsp White Pepper Powder
1/8 Tsp Black Pepper Powder
1/2 Tsp Salt
1/8 Tsp Sugar

Directions
1. In a medium bowl, combine the chicken and marinade ingredients, making sure to completely coat the chicken. Allow to sit for an hour
2. In a small bowl, pour in the whisked egg. Place the cornstarch in a separate bowl
3. Coat the marinated chicken in egg, then in cornstarch and set aside
4. Preheat the Air Fryer to 375 degrees
5. Place the chicken pieces into the Air Fryer tray and cook for 20 minutes
6. Whilst hot, sprinkle the basil and five spice powder on top of the chicken and toss to coat
7. Serve immediately while chicken is still crispy

TUNA BITES

Ingredients
14 Ozs Canned Tuna
2 Sheets Puff Pastry
1 Onion
2 Green Chilies
Small Knob of Ginger
1/2 Cup Coriander
2 Tsps Pepper
2 Cups Cabbage
Salt to taste

Directions
1. Preheat the Air Fryer to 390 degrees
2. Finely chop the onion, chilies, ginger and cabbage. Mix the ingredients together excluding the puff pastry sheet
3. Roll out the puff pastry and cut into large rectangles
4. Fill the puff pastry with the tuna mixture and seal the final edge
5. Place the pastry bites into the Air Fryer tray to cook for 15 minutes. Check after 10 minutes as cooking time will depend on thickness of pastry
6. The bites are ready when they are crispy and puffed. Serve with a side salad

VEGETABLE CHIPS

Ingredients
2 Taros
2 Yams
2 Parsnips
1/2 Tsp Salt

Directions
1. Peel each vegetable and wash, then pat dry. Using a slicer, slice the vegetables very thinly, about 1/8 inch thick
2. Preheat the Air Fryer to 320 degrees
3. Fry the vegetable slices a handful at a time in the Air Fryer tray for 2 minutes until lightly browned and crispy. Shake the tray for a more even cooking result
4. Sprinkle with salt while still warm, and continue frying in batches

VEGETABLE SPRING ROLLS

Ingredients
For the filling:
2 Cups Cabbage
1 Carrot
1 Onion
2 Inch Piece Ginger
8 Cloves Garlic
1 Tsp Sugar
1 Tbsp White Pepper Powder
1 Tsp Soy Sauce
Salt to taste

For the wrapping:
16 Spring Roll Sheets
2 Tbsps Corn Flour

Directions
1. Grate the cabbage into shreds. Chop the carrot and onion into thin strips
2. Mince the ginger and garlic very finely and combine all filling ingredients into a bowl and mix thoroughly
3. In a separate bowl, mix the corn flour and add some water slowly until a cream like paste is created
4. Take a sheet of the spring roll wrapper and place a tablespoon of stuffing in one corner. Roll it tight and fold the sides inwards. Shape into a cylinder and apply a smear of the corn flour paste to adhere
5. Repeat the same process with all the sheets and arrange them on a plate
6. Preheat the Air Fryer to 350 degrees and cook spring rolls in batches for 20 minutes
7. Serve whilst crispy

ZUCCHINI PATTIES

Ingredients
2 Cups Zucchini
1 Cup Parmesan Cheese, shredded
Salt and Pepper to season
1/4 Cup Onion, diced
1/2 Cup Flour
2 Eggs

Directions
1. Grate the zucchini using a box grater
2. Preheat the Air Fryer at 350 degrees
3. In a medium bowl, combine the zucchini, eggs, onion, flour, Parmesan, and salt and pepper. Stir well to distribute ingredients evenly
4. Shape the mixture into four small patties
5. Cook patties in the Air Fryer for 8 minutes until crispy to touch
6. Serve with tomato relish

MAIN MEALS

BALSAMIC GARLIC CHICKEN BREAST

Ingredients
4 Chicken Breasts
Salt and Pepper
3/4 lb Mushrooms, sliced
2 Tbsps Flour
2 Tbsps Vegetable Oil
5 Cloves Garlic, minced
1/4 Cup Balsamic Vinegar
1 Cup Chicken Broth
1 Bay Leaf
1/4 Tsp Thyme
1 Tbsp Butter
* Baking Dish

Directions
1. Cut the breasts into even slices and season with salt and pepper
2. Add some additional seasoning to the flour, then coat the chicken slices well
3. Preheat the Air Fryer at 350 degrees
4. Layer chicken pieces into the baking dish. Place the dish into the Air Fryer tray and cook for 20 minutes
5. Open the tray and toss in mushrooms and minced garlic. Cook for a further 2 minutes and then pour in the chicken broth, balsamic, bay leaf and thyme
6. After 10 minutes, transfer remove the tray and Discard the bay leaf
7. Serve with a side salad or vegetables

BBQ PORK FOR SANDWICHES

Ingredients
14 Oz Can Beef Broth
3 lbs Boneless Pork Ribs
Barbeque Sauce
* Baking Tray

Directions
1. Pour the can of beef broth into a slow cooker, and add the pork ribs. Cook on high heat for 4 hours, or until meat shreds easily
2. Remove meat and shred with two forks
3. Preheat the Air Fryer at 350 degrees
4. Transfer the shredded pork to a baking tray and stir in the barbeque sauce
5. Place the tray in the Air Fryer to cook for 30 minutes, or until heated through

BEEF BURGERS

Ingredients
1 lb Ground Beef
1 Tbsp Worcestershire sauce
1 Tsp Soy Sauce
1/2 Tsp Garlic Powder
1/2 Tsp Onion Powder
1/2 Tsp Salt
1/2 Tsp Black Pepper
1/2 Tsp Dried Oregano
1 Tsp Dried Parsley

Directions
1. In a small bowl, mix together all the ingredients until well combined
2. Divide the beef mixture into four and shape into patties. With your thumb, put an indent in the center of each one to prevent the patties bunching up in the middle
3. Preheat the Air Fryer to 390 degrees
4. Place patties in the Air Fryer tray and cook for 12 minutes for medium or longer to desired degree of doneness
5. Serve hot on a hamburger bun

BEEF SCHNITZEL

Ingredients
1 Beef Schnitzel
2 Tbsps Vegetable Oil
1/3 Cup Breadcrumbs
1 Egg, whisked
1 Lemon, to serve

Directions
1. Preheat Air Fryer to 350 degrees
2. Mix the oil and the breadcrumbs together. Keep stirring until the mixture becomes loose and crumbly
3. Dip the schnitzel into the egg and then into the crumb mix, making sure it is evenly and fully covered
4. Gently lay the schnitzel in the Air Fryer and cook for 12 minutes or until brown and crispy
5. Serve with lemon drizzled over the top

BEEF STROGANOFF

Ingredients
9 Ozs Tender Beef
1 Onion, chopped
1 Tbsp Paprika
3/4 Cup Sour Cream
Salt and Pepper to taste
* Baking Dish

Directions
1. Preheat the Air Fryer to 390 degrees
2. Chop the beef and marinate it with the paprika
3. Add the chopped onions into the baking dish and heat for about 2 minutes in the Air Fryer
4. When the onions are transparent, add the beef into the dish and cook for 5 minutes
5. Once the beef is starting to tender, pour in the sour cream and cook for another 7 minutes
6. At this point, the liquid should have reduced. Season with salt and pepper and serve

BEEF WITH BEANS

Ingredients
12 Ozs Lean Steak
1 Onion, sliced
1 Can Chopped Tomatoes
3/4 Cup Beef Stock
4 Tsp Fresh Thyme, chopped
1 Can Red Kidney Beans
Salt and Pepper to taste
* Oven Safe Bowl

Directions
1. Preheat the Air Fryer to 390 degrees
2. Trim the fat from the meat and cut into thin 1cm strips
3. Add onion slices to the oven safe bowl and place in the Air Fryer. Cook for 3 minutes
4. Add the meat and continue cooking for 5 minutes
5. Add the tomatoes and their juice, beef stock, thyme and the beans and cook for an additional 5 minutes
6. Season with black pepper to taste

BLACK BEAN VEGGIE BURGERS

Ingredients
16 Oz Can Black Beans
1/2 Bell Pepper, diced
1/2 Onion, chopped
2 Cloves Garlic, minced
1 Egg
1 Tbsp Chili Powder
1 Tbsp Cumin
1 Tsp Hot Sauce
1/2 Cup Breadcrumbs

Directions
1. Heat the Air Fryer to 390 degrees
2. Drain the black beans and place them in a large bowl. Use a masher to compress the beans until they form a thick paste
3. Add all the remaining ingredients to the bowl and combine well. The mixture should be firm and sticky
4. Divide the mixture into 4 even portions and form into veggie patties
5. Place patties into the Air Fryer and cook for 15 to 18 minutes until crispy

BOLOGNAISE SAUCE

Ingredients
13 Ozs Ground Beef
1 Carrot
1 Stalk of Celery
10 Ozs Diced Tomatoes
1/2 Onion
Salt and Pepper to taste
*Oven safe bowl

Directions
1. Preheat the Air Fryer to 390 degrees
2. Finely dice the carrot, celery and onions. Place into the oven safe bowl along with the ground beef and combine well
3. Place the bowl into the Air Fryer tray and cook for 12 minutes until browned
4. Pour the diced tomatoes into the bowl and replace in the Air Fryer. Season with salt and pepper, then cook for another 18 minutes
5. Serve over cooked pasta or freeze for later use

BREADED SPAM STEAKS

Ingredients
12 Oz Can Luncheon Meat
1 Cup All Purpose Flour
2 Eggs, beaten
2 Cups Italian Seasoned Breadcrumbs

Directions
1. Preheat the Air Fryer to 380 degrees
2. Cut the luncheon meat into 1/4 inch slices
3. Gently press the luncheon meat slices into the flour to coat and shake off the excess flour. Dip into the beaten egg, then press into breadcrumbs
4. Place the battered slices into the Air Fryer tray and cook for 3 to 5 minutes until golden brown
5. Serve with chili or tomato sauce

CAJUN CORN MEAL BREADED CHICKEN

Ingredients
2 Chicken Breasts, cut into even strips
1 Cup Self Rising Corn Meal Mix
1 ½ Cups Plain Flour
4 Tsps Cajun Seasoning
1/2 Tsp Salt
1 ½ Cups Buttermilk
1 Tsp Chili Sauce

Directions
1. Combine the Cajun seasoning, salt, corn meal and half a cup of the plain flour in a bowl
2. Mix the chili sauce and buttermilk in another bowl
3. Take each chicken strip and dip into the remaining flour, then into the buttermilk, and finally into the Cajun mixture. Repeat twice for additional coating
4. Preheat the Air Fryer to 350 degrees
5. Place the battered chicken strips in the Air Fryer tray and cook for 15 minutes until golden brown
6. Serve hot with tomato relish

CARAMEL APPLE PORK CHOPS

Ingredients
4 Pork Chops
2 Apples, peeled and sliced
2 Tbsps Brown Sugar
Salt and Pepper
1/8 Tsp Ground Cinnamon
1/8 Tsp Ground Nutmeg
2 Tbsps Butter, melted

Directions
1. Preheat Air Fryer at 390 degrees
2. Season the chops with salt and pepper and place into the Air Fryer. Cook for 13 minutes then allow to rest under some foil
3. In a pan, simmer the apple, butter, sugar, salt and pepper, cinnamon and nutmeg. Cook for about 8 minutes until apple slices are softened
4. Pour the caramel apple sauce over the cooked chops to serve

CHAR SIEW PORK

Ingredients
9 Ozs Pork Shoulder
1 Tbsp Hoisin Sauce
1/2 Tbsp Oyster Sauce
1 Tsp Light Soy Sauce
1/2 Tsp Dark Soy Sauce
1 Tsp Chinese Cooking Wine
1/2 Tsp Sesame Oil
1/2 Tbsp Honey
1/2 Tbsp Sugar
1 Tsp Garlic Powder
1/4 Tsp Chinese Five Spice Powder
Dash of White Pepper

Directions
1. Slice the shoulder meat into 2 long pieces
2. Marinate the pork with all seasoning ingredients and allow to sit overnight in the fridge
3. Preheat the Air Fryer at 390 degrees
4. Place the marinated pork into the Air Fryer tray and cook for 10 minutes. At 5 minutes, baste with additional marinating sauce
5. Reduce the temperature to 320 degrees and cook for another 15 minutes until lightly charred. Continue to baste at flip the pork at intervals of 5 minutes until fully cooked
6. Allow the char siew to cook slightly and then slice
7. Serve with white rice

CHEESY PAPRIKA CHICKEN

Ingredients
4 Chicken Breasts
4 Ozs Firm Cheese, sliced into sticks
2 Tsps Paprika
1 Tsp Thyme
1 Sliced Onion
2/3 Cup Tomato Juice
2/3 Cup Chicken Stock
2 Cloves Garlic, minced
10 Basil Leaves
2 Tsp Olive Oil
Salt and Pepper to taste
Kitchen String
* Oven Safe Bowl

Directions
1. Preheat the Air Fryer to 390 degrees
2. Cut the chicken breast in half lengthwise. Season with salt and pepper and place a stick of cheese in the middle. Close and tie with kitchen string like a roast
3. Add the onion and garlic into the oven safe bowl and cook in the Air Fryer for 5 minutes until soft
4. Mix olive oil with the paprika and brush the chicken. Add the thyme and chicken to the bowl over the cooked onion and garlic. Heat for another 6 minutes
5. Pull open the Air Fryer tray and add the tomato juice and chicken stock. Cook for 6 more minutes
6. Adjust seasoning in the sauce, remove the string from the chicken and serve with vegetables

CHEESY TURKEY MEATLOAF

Ingredients

2 lbs Ground Turkey

1 Cup Milk
1 Cup Italian Seasoned Breadcrumbs
2 Eggs
1 Tsp Salt
1/4 Tsp Pepper
3/4 lb Colby Cheese, cubed
1/2 Cup Ketchup
* Small Loaf Baking Tray

Directions
1. Preheat the Air Fryer at 390 degrees
2. In a bowl, mix the turkey, milk, breadcrumbs, and eggs by hand. Season with salt and pepper
3. Fold the cheese cubes into the mixture. Transfer to the loaf pan and top with ketchup
4. Place the pan into the Air Fryer and cook for 45 minutes or until the loaf is no longer pink in the middle

CHICKEN LIME TAQUITOS

Ingredients
4 Chicken Breasts, halved
1/4 Cup Roasted Red Peppers, julienned
1/3 Cup Shredded Monterey Jack Cheese
1/2 Tsp Garlic Powder
1 Tsp Chili Powder
1/4 Cup Lime Juice
2 Tsps Minced Garlic
1/4 Cup Onion, sliced
18 Corn Tortillas
1/8 Cup Oil
1 ½ Tsp Salt

Directions
1. Combine the chicken, 1 teaspoon of salt, chili powder, garlic powder and oil in a bowl. Marinate the chicken in mixture for at least 2 hours
2. Preheat the Air Fryer to 350 degrees
3. Drain chicken well and cook in the Air Fryer for 25 minutes. Allow to cool and shred the meat into small pieces
4. Place chicken in bowl and sprinkle with remaining ½ teaspoon of salt and minced garlic. Mix well. Then add red pepper, onion, cheese and lime juice, combining thoroughly
5. To assemble, heat tortillas in a microwave until soft and pliable. Spoon 2 ounces of chicken filling over the tortilla and roll tightly, securing with a toothpick
6. Serve with guacamole and salsa

CHICKEN TIKKA

Ingredients
2 Chicken Breasts, cut into 1-inch cubes
1/2 Cup Greek yogurt
1 Tbsp Olive Oil
4 Tbsps Melted Butter
1 Onion Diced
2 Tsps Grated Ginger
1 Tsps Minced Garlic
1 Can Diced Tomatoes
1 Tbsp Garam Masala
1/4 Tsp Cayenne Pepper
1/2 Cup Thickened Cream
Salt and Pepper to taste

Directions
1. Clean, wash and pat dry chicken.
2. Mix all the ingredients except for the butter together and marinate the chicken for 2 hours or overnight if time permits
3. Preheat the Air Fryer to 350 degrees
4. Brush the chicken with melted butter so it is evenly coated
5. Place pieces into Air Fryer tray and cook for 12 minutes or until the surface starts browning
6. Serve hot with naan or basmati rice

CHIMICHURRI STEAK

Ingredients
1 lb Skirt Steak
1 Cup Parsley, finely chopped
1/4 Cup Mint, finely chopped
2 Tbsps Oregano, finely chopped
3 Garlic Cloves, finely chopped
1 Tsp Red Pepper Powder
1 Tbsp Ground Cumin
1 Tsp Cayenne Pepper
2 Tsps Smoked Paprika
1/4 Tsp Black Pepper
3/4 Cup Olive Oil
3 Tbsps Red Wine Vinegar
1 Tsp Salt

Directions
1. Combine all ingredients except for the steak in a bowl to form the chimichurri
2. Cut the steak into 2 portions and add to a re-sealable bag, along with a quarter cup of the chimichurri. Refrigerate for 2 hours or preferably overnight
3. Preheat the Air Fryer to 350 degrees
4. Pat steak dry with a paper towel and add to the cooking tray
5. Cook for 10 minutes for medium-rare or longer depending on preference
6. Garnish with remaining chimichurri on top and serve

CHINESE BRAISED PORK BELLY

Ingredients
1 lb Pork Belly, sliced
1 Tbsp Oyster Sauce
1 Tbsp Sugar
2 Red Fermented Bean Curds
1 Tbsp Red Fermented Bean Curd Paste
1 Tbsp Cooking Wine
1/2 Tbsp Soy Sauce
1 Tsp Sesame Oil
1 Cup All Purpose Flour

Directions
1. Preheat the Air Fryer to 390 degrees
2. In a small bowl, mix all ingredients together and rub the pork thoroughly with this mixture
3. Set aside to marinate for at least 30 minutes or preferably overnight for the flavors to permeate the meat
4. Coat each marinated pork belly slice in flour and place in the Air Fryer tray
5. Cook for 15 to 20 minutes until crispy and tender

CHINESE PORK RIBS

Ingredients
1 Rack of Pork Ribs
1/3 Tsp Baking Soda
1 Tbsp Water
1/2 Tsp Salt
1 Tsp Sugar
1 Tbsp Soy Sauce
1 Tbsp Cornstarch
1/4 Tsp Sesame Oil
1 Tbsp Minced Garlic
1 Tsp Five Spice Powder

Directions
1. Preheat the Air Fryer to 390 degrees
2. Cut ribs into single sections and place in a bowl. Add the remaining ingredients and coat each rib evenly
3. Marinate for a least 1 hour or preferably overnight
4. Add ribs to the Air Fryer and cook for 20 to 25 minutes until tender

CHIPOTLE CHICKEN

Ingredients
2 Chicken Breasts, halved
1 Cup Breadcrumbs
1/4 Cup Parmesan, shredded
1/2 Tsp Garlic Salt
Black Pepper to taste
1/2 Cup Mayonnaise
2 Chipotle Chilies in Adobo Sauce

Directions
1. In a medium bowl, mix the Parmesan, garlic salt, breadcrumbs, and black pepper together
2. In a food processor, combine the mayonnaise and chipotle chilies until there are no lumps. Coat the chicken breasts with this mixture, ensuring that all sides are covered
3. Dip each coated breast into the Parmesan mix and set aside for 10 minutes to firm in the freezer
4. Preheat the Air Fryer to 350 degrees
5. Place the chicken breast halves into the Air Fryer tray and cook for about 20 to 25 minutes until browned and cooked through

COCONUT CORIANDER TILAPIA

Ingredients
4 Tilapia Fillets
Salt to season
1/2 Cup Coconut Milk
1/2 Cup Coriander
1 Tsp Ginger
1/2 Tsp Garam Masala
3 Garlic Cloves
1/2 Jalapeno Pepper, seeds removed
Cooking Spray
* Baking Dish

Directions
1. Preheat the Air Fryer to 390 degrees
2. Grease the baking dish with the cooking spray. Lightly salt the tilapia fillets to season and position in the dish
3. In a food processor, pulse the remaining ingredients together until it forms a smooth consistency. Cover the tilapia with the mixture
4. Place the dish into the Air Fryer and cook for 12 to 14 minutes until the fish is just done
5. Serve hot over rice

COCONUT SHRIMP

Ingredients
4 Jumbo Prawns, deveined
1 Cup Desiccated Coconut
1/2 Tsp Ginger Garlic Paste
1/2 Tsp White Pepper Powder
1 Tbsp Coriander Leaves, chopped
1 Tbsp Curry Leaf, chopped
1/2 Cup Lemon Juice
Pinch of Turmeric
1 Tsp Chili Powder
2 Tsps Flour
Salt to taste
1 Egg

Directions
1. In a mixing bowl, add the flour, lemon juice, ginger garlic paste, turmeric, pepper, chili powder, coriander leaves, curry leaves, salt and egg. Combine well
2. Dip the jumbo prawns in the marinade and coat well on all sides
3. Remove and coat with desiccated coconut
4. Preheat the Air Fryer at 350 degrees
5. Place the prawns in the tray and fry them for 8 minutes
6. Remove and serve with any sauce

COCONUT TUMERIC CHICKEN

Ingredients
3 Chicken Legs
1/4 Cup Coconut Milk
4 Tsp Ground Turmeric
3 Tbsps Old Ginger, minced
3 Tbsps Galangal, minced
1/2 Tbsp Salt

Directions
1. Cut a few slits on the chicken legs to help in absorbing the flavor when marinating
2. Combine the remaining ingredients in a bowl and mix thoroughly
3. Place chicken legs into the bowl mixture and leave it to marinate for at least 4 hours or overnight in the refrigerator
4. Preheat the Air Fryer to 375 degrees
5. Cook the chicken for 20 to 25 minutes and flip over at half-time
6. The chicken is ready when it is golden brown and crispy

CRISPY ROAST PORK

Ingredients
9 Ozs Pork Belly
2 Tsps Garlic Salt
1 Tsp Five Spice Powder
1 Tsp Ground Pepper
Salt to taste
1 Lemon

Directions
1. Boil the pork belly until it is cooked through
2. Remove from water and allow to air dry in the open (around 3 hours). Pluck excess hair if any
3. Prepare the pork by pricking the skin all over with a sharp skewer. This will help the pork to crisp up during cooking
4. Lightly score the skin with a knife
5. Combine the spices and then massage the dry rub into the scored meat
6. Cut the lemon and rub the juice on the skin. Follow with a generous sprinkling of salt
7. Preheat the Air Fryer at 350 degrees
8. Place the pork belly skin facing upwards in the tray. Air fry for 45 minutes and check for desired crispness
9. Continue cooking for another 10 minutes if you prefer tough crackling

CRUMBED FISH

Ingredients
4 White Fish Fillets
4 Tbsps Vegetable Oil
1/2 Cup Breadcrumbs
1 Egg, whisked
1 Lemon

Directions
1. Preheat the Air Fryer to 350 degrees
2. Mix the oil and the breadcrumbs together. Keep stirring until the mixture becomes loose and crumbly
3. Dip the fish fillets into the egg and then into the crumb mix making sure it is evenly covered
4. Gently lay in the Air Fryer then cook for 12 minutes
5. Serve immediately with lemon

DIJONAISE SALMON

Ingredients
4 Salmon Fillets
1/4 Cup Butter, melted
3 Tbsps Dijon Mustard
1 ½ Tbsps Honey
1/4 Cup Breadcrumbs
1/4 Cup Pecans
4 Tsps Parsley
Salt and Pepper to taste

Directions
1. Preheat the Air Fryer at 375 degrees
2. Combine the mustard, butter and honey in a bowl
3. Finely dice the pecans and parsley, then combine with the breadcrumbs in a separate bowl
4. Dredge each fillet into the mustard mix, then coat in the pecan mixture
5. Place coated fillets into the Air Fryer and cook for 12 minutes until just tender and browned
6. Sprinkle with salt and pepper to serve

FINGER STEAKS

Ingredients
2 lbs Flat Iron Steaks
1 Cup All Purpose Flour
3 Tsps Seasoned Salt
1 Tsp Black Pepper
1/4 Cup Buttermilk
1/4 Cup Dark Beer or Ale
1 Tbsp Hot Pepper Sauce
1 Egg

Directions
1. Whisk the flour, salt and pepper together in a mixing bowl. Beat the egg in a separate mixing bowl, then mix in the buttermilk, beer, and hot pepper sauce until smooth
2. Cut the steak into strips which will fit into the Air Fryer tray
3. Gently press the steak strips into the flour to coat and shake off the excess flour. Place the steak strips into the beaten egg, then toss in the flour again
4. Place onto a baking sheet, and freeze until solid for about 4 hours
5. Preheat the Air Fryer to 340 degrees
6. Fry the frozen steak strips in batches until the breading is golden brown, and the beef has cooked to your desired degree of doneness. After 5 minutes of cooking, the steak should be medium cooked depending on the size of the strips

FISH AND CHIPS

Ingredients
7 Ozs White Fish Fillet
2 Tbsps Tortilla Chips
11 Ozs Potatoes
1 Tbsp Vegetable Oil
1/2 Tbsp Lemon Juice
1 Egg

Directions
1. Preheat the Air Fryer to 350 degrees
2. Cut the fish into four equal pieces and rub with lemon juice, salt, and pepper
3. Pulse the tortilla chips to fine pieces in a food processor and transfer to a plate. Beat the egg in a separate bowl
4. Dip the pieces of fish into the egg one by one and then roll through the ground tortilla chips so that they are evenly covered
5. Scrub the potatoes clean and cut them lengthwise into thin strips. Soak the potato strips in water for at least 30 minutes. Drain thoroughly and then pat them dry. Coat the dried strips with oil
6. Place the marinated fish and potatoes into the Air Fryer tray. Set the timer to 12 minutes and fry the potatoes and the fish until they are crispy brown

FRIED CHICKEN CUTLET

Ingredients
4 Pieces Boneless Chicken Thigh
1 Cup Flour
2 Eggs, beaten
1 Cup Panko Breadcrumbs
2 Pinches of Salt and Pepper
Cooking Spray

Directions
1. Mix the salt and pepper into the breadcrumbs
2. Taking each thigh piece, coat the chicken in flour, egg, then into the breadcrumb mixture
3. Cook the battered cutlets in the Air Fryer for 20 minutes at 350 degrees
4. Turn the cutlets at the 20 minute point and then cook for another 5 minutes at 390 degrees for extra crispy texture
5. Serve with preferred dipping sauce

FRIED QUAIL WITH SPICY SALT

Ingredients
4 Quails
1 Tsp Sugar
1 Tbsp Light Soy Sauce
1 Tbsp Rice Wine
3 Tbsps All Purpose Flour

For the Salt and Pepper mix:
4 Tsps Salt
2 Tsps Szechuan Peppercorns, crushed
1 Tsp Chinese Five Spice Powder

Directions
1. To make the spicy salt and pepper, combine the ingredients and dry fry in a pan over a low heat for 2 to 3 minutes or until aromatic
2. Split each quail in half down the middle and clean well
3. Marinate with the spicy salt and pepper, sugar, soy and rice wine for a minimum of 2 hours in the refrigerator
4. Heat the Air Fryer to 350 degrees
5. Coat each quail piece in flour, dusting off the excess
6. Fry the quail for 10 minutes or until crispy
7. Serve with the lemon wedges on the side

GARLIC LAMB CHOPS

Ingredients
8 Lamb Chops
1 Garlic Bulb
3 Tbsps Olive Oil
1 Tbsp Oregano, finely chopped
Salt and Pepper to taste

Directions
1. Preheat the Air Fryer to 390 degrees
2. Thinly coat the garlic bulb with olive oil and put it in the Air Fryer for 12 minutes to roast
3. In a bowl, mix the herbs with some salt, pepper and olive oil. Thinly coat the lamb chops with half a tablespoon of herb oil and marinate for 10 minutes
4. Remove the garlic and place lamb chops in the Air Fryer for 5 minutes. Roast the chops until nicely brown but pink on the inside. Rest under some tin foil whilst you are cooking in batches
5. Squeeze the garlic cloves between your thumb and index finger over the herb oil. Add some salt and pepper, and stir the mixture well
6. Serve the lamb chops with a chili or mint sauce for extra flavor

GARLIC MARINATED STEAK

Ingredients
2 Rib Eye Steaks
1/2 Cup Balsamic Vinegar
1/4 Cup Soy Sauce
3 Tbsps Garlic, diced
2 Tbsps Honey
1 Tbsp Vegetable Oil
Salt and Pepper to taste
1 Tsp Worcestershire Sauce
1 Tsp Onion Powder
1/4 Tsp Cayenne Pepper

Directions
1. Combine all ingredients except for the rib eye steaks in a large bowl
2. Once the mixture is well combined, place the steaks into the bowl to marinate. Cover with cling film and place in the refrigerator overnight
3. Preheat the Air Fryer at 390 degrees
4. Cook the steaks for 14 to 16 minutes for a medium done outcome
5. Serve with a side of vegetables

GINGER BEEF

Ingredients
1 lb Beef Steak
3/4 Cup Cornstarch
1/2 Cup Water
2 Eggs
1 Carrot, julienned
1/4 Cup Onion, diced
1/4 Cup Ginger, minced
5 Garlic Cloves, minced
1 Tbsp Sesame Oil
4 Tbsps White Vinegar
3 Tbsps Soy Sauce
1/2 Cup Sugar
3 Tsps Red Pepper Flakes

Directions
1. Trim excess fat from the beef and cut into narrow strips up to 2 ½ inches long
2. Place cornstarch in a bowl and add water gradually while whisking. Beat the eggs into the mixture
3. Toss the beef into the bowl and stir to coat
4. Heat the Air Fryer to 390 degrees
5. Cook the coated beef strips in the Air Fryer for 12 to 15 minutes or until crispy. Remove strips to rest under foil
6. Combine the sesame oil, carrots, onion, ginger, and garlic in the Air Fryer tray and cook for another 8 minutes
7. Add the vinegar, soy sauce, pepper flakes and sugar into the vegetable mixture. Cook for another 6 minutes until the sauce has thickened
8. Pour over the beef strips and serve

GINGER GLAZED MAHI MAHI

Ingredients
4 Mahi Mahi Fillets
3 Tbsps Honey
3 Tbsps Soy Sauce
3 Tbsps Balsamic Vinegar
1 Tsp Grated Ginger
2 Cloves Garlic, minced
2 Tsps Olive Oil
Salt and Pepper

Directions
1. Preheat the Air Fryer at 350 degrees
2. In a bowl, combine the honey, ginger, soy sauce, vinegar, garlic and oil. Sprinkle the fillets with salt and pepper and place in the bowl to marinate. Cover with cling film and place in the refrigerator for at least one hour
3. Remove fish from the bowl and reserve the sauce. Cook the marinated fillets in the Air Fryer for 10 minutes
4. Pour the sauce into a pan and simmer until it forms a thickened glaze
5. Serve over cooked fish

GREEK KEFTEDE MEATBALLS

Ingredients
2 lbs Ground Beef
1/4 Cup Lemon Juice
4 Potatoes, peeled
1 Onion, grated
3/4 Cup Breadcrumbs
1 Cup Parsley, chopped
1/3 Cup Mint
1/2 Tsp Ground Cinnamon
2 Tsps Lemon Zest
2 Eggs, whisked
1 Tbsp Salt
1 Tsp Black Pepper

Directions
1. Preheat the Air Fryer to 390 degrees
2. Grate the potatoes into a bowl. Add the remaining ingredients and combine well
3. Taking heaped spoonfuls of the mixture, roll into small balls of even size
4. Place meatballs into the Air Fryer tray in batches, ensuring that they do not overlap. Cook for 8 to 10 minutes until browned
5. Serve with lemon wedges

GRILLED SALMON

Ingredients
2 Salmon Fillets
1/2 Tsp Lemon Pepper
1/2 Tsp Garlic Powder
Salt and Pepper
1/3 Cup Soy Sauce
1/3 Cup Sugar
1 Tbsp Olive Oil

Directions
1. Season salmon fillets with lemon pepper, garlic powder and salt
2. In a shallow bowl, add a third cup of water and combine the olive oil, soy sauce and sugar
3. Place salmon the bowl and immerse in the sauce. Cover with cling film and allow to marinate in the refrigerator for at least an hour
4. Preheat the Air Fryer at 350 degrees
5. Place salmon into the Air Fryer and cook for 10 minutes or more until the fish is tender
6. Serve with lemon wedges

HONEY GLAZED SALMON

Ingredients
2 Salmon Fillets
6 Tbsps Honey
6 Tsps Soy Sauce
3 Tsps Rice Wine Vinegar
1 Tsp Water

Directions
1. Mix honey, soy sauce, rice wine and water together
2. Pour half of the mixture in a separate bowl and set aside. This will be used as a sauce to serve with the salmon
3. Place the salmon into the remaining mixture. Allow to marinate for at least 2 hours or overnight
4. Preheat the Air Fryer at 350 degrees
5. Cook the salmon for 8 minutes, flip over halfway and continue with additional 5 minutes. Baste with additional sauce when flipping if desired
6. Serve hot with reserved sauce

HONEY MUSTARD CHICKEN

Ingredients
2 Chicken Breasts, halved
1/3 Cup Dijon Mustard
1/3 Cup Honey
2 Tbsps Mayonnaise
1 Tsp Ketchup
1/2 Tsp Worcestershire Sauce

Directions
1. Combine the ketchup, Worcestershire, mustard, honey and mayonnaise in a bowl. Reserve a tablespoon of the sauce for basting. Coat the breasts in the remaining sauce
2. Cover with cling film. Allow the chicken to marinate in the fridge for at least 30 minutes
3. Preheat Air Fryer at 350 degrees
4. Place the marinated chicken into the Air Fryer to cook for 22 to 25 minutes
5. Open the tray and baste with the reserved sauce. Cook for another 5 to 10 minutes depending on the thickness of the chicken breast
6. Serve over white rice

HONEY SESAME PRAWNS

Ingredients
24 King Prawns, peeled with tails intact
3/4 Cup Iced Water
1 Egg, Lightly Whisked
2 Tbsps Sesame Seeds
3/4 Cup Self Raising Flour
1/4 Tsp Salt
1/2 Cup Honey

Directions
1. Preheat the Air Fryer to 350 degrees
2. Combine the water, egg and half the sesame seeds in a bowl. Add the flour and salt, and whisk until just combined
3. Place the prawns, one at a time, into the batter
4. Add to the Air Fryer and cook for 5 minutes or until golden and cooked through
5. In a saucepan, heat the honey over medium heat for one minute or until melted. Add the fried prawns and cook for another minute
6. Sprinkle honeyed prawns with the remaining sesame seeds. Drizzle with pan juices and serve immediately

ITALIAN BREADED PORK CHOPS

Ingredients
4 Pork Chops
3 Eggs, whisked
3 Tbsps Milk
1 ½ Cups Italian Seasoned Breadcrumbs
1/2 Cup Parmesan Cheese, shredded
2 Tbsps Dried Parsley
2 Tbsps Olive Oil
4 Cloves Garlic, minced

Directions
1. Preheat Air Fryer at 390 degrees
2. Mix the eggs and milk together in a bowl. In another bowl, combine the Parmesan, garlic, parsley, and breadcrumbs
3. Cover each pork chop in the egg and milk, then place in the Parmesan mixture. Repeat twice for each pork chop
4. Place coated pork chops in the Air Fryer, and cook for 15 minutes or until done. Turn the chops halfway through

ITALIAN SAUSAGE AND PEPPERS

Ingredients
1 lb Italian Link Sausage
1 Onion
2 Bell Peppers
Pinch of Salt
1/2 Cup Tomato Sauce
Parsley or Basil for garnish
* Oven Safe Bowl

Directions
1. Preheat the Air Fryer to 390 degrees
2. Cut the link sausages in half, place them in the oven safe bowl then cook in the Air Fryer for 10 minutes
3. Slice the onion and peppers, then add them to the Air Fryer over the sausages with a pinch of salt. Cook for another 10 minutes
4. In the last 2 minutes, pour in the tomato sauce to simmer flavors together gently
5. Serve garnished with parsley or basil

ITALIAN STYLE FISH

Ingredients
4 Trout Fillets
2 Tbsps Olive Oil
1 Tbsp Butter
1 lb Mushrooms, sliced
2 Cloves Garlic, minced
2 Tbsps Green Onions, sliced
2 Tbsps, Fresh Parsley, chopped
Salt and Pepper to taste
4 Tbsp Italian Style Breadcrumbs
Cooking Spray
Lemon Wedges to serve
* Baking Dish

Directions
1. Preheat the Air Fryer to 375 degrees
2. Grease the baking dish with cooking spray. Add sliced mushrooms, onions, one tablespoon of parsley and garlic
3. Arrange fish in the dish. Brush with olive oil and then season with salt and pepper
4. Melt the butter and toss with breadcrumbs. Sprinkle over fish
5. Place into the Air Fryer and bake for 15 to 20 minutes, or until fish is tender inside and crumbs are lightly golden
6. Sprinkle with remaining parsley, and garnish with lemon wedges

KEY WEST CHICKEN

Ingredients
2 Chicken Breasts, halved
3 Tbsps Soy Sauce
1 Tbsp Honey
1 Tbsp Olive Oil
1 Tsp Lemon Juice
2 Tsps Garlic, minced

Directions
1. Combine the oil, soy sauce, honey, lemon juice, and garlic in a bowl
2. Place chicken into the bowl and ensure that each halve is covered in the marinade. Allow to marinate in the refrigerator overnight for depth of flavor
3. Preheat the Air Fryer at 375 degrees
4. Place the marinated chicken into the Air Fryer tray and cook for 18 to 22 minutes until cooked through

KOREAN STYLE CHICKEN TENDERS

Ingredients
1 lb Chicken Tenderloins
1/2 Cup Soy Sauce
1/2 Cup Pineapple Juice
1/4 Cup Sesame Oil
6 Garlic Cloves, chopped
4 Scallions, chopped
1 Tbsp Grated Ginger
2 Tsps Toasted Sesame Seeds
* Bamboo Skewers

Directions
1. Skewer each chicken tender, trimming excess meat or fat
2. Combine all other ingredients in a large mixing bowl. Add the skewered chicken to the bowl, mix well and refrigerate, covered, for a minimum of 2 hours or overnight
3. Preheat the Air Fryer to 390 degrees
4. Pat chicken completely dry with a paper towel. Add half of the skewers to the Air Fryer tray and cook each batch for 10 to 12 minutes
5. Serve with pickled vegetables or mustard based sauce

LAMB KIBBEH

Ingredients
11 Ozs Minced Lamb
1 Cup Cooked Burghul
1 Onion, chopped
1 Tbsp Vegetable Oil
2 Tbsps Pine Nuts

Directions
1. In a food processor, pulse 9 ounces of the lamb until it has a smooth texture. Combine with the prepared burghul in a bowl along with half of the chopped onion
2. In a pan, heat the oil and cook the remaining 2 ounces of lamb for 3 minutes. Toss in the pine nuts and remaining onion and cook for another minute. Remove from heat and set aside until the mixture has cooled
3. Take large spoonfuls of the burghul and roll into balls. Using your thumb, make an indent in the center of each kibbeh ball and they fill with the cooled lamb mixture. Smooth the top of the burghul over the ball to enclose
4. Preheat the Air Fryer to 350 degrees
5. Place kibbeh into the Air Fryer tray and cook in batches for 7 minutes until crispy
6. Serve with a yoghurt based sauce

LEMON ROSEMARY CHICKEN

Ingredients
For the Chicken:
12 Ozs Chicken Breast, sliced
1 Tsp Ginger, minced
1 Tbsp Soy Sauce
1/2 Tbsp Olive Oil

For the Sauce:
1/2 Lemon, cut in wedges
1 Tbsp Rosemary, chopped
3 Tbsps Sugar
1 Tbsp Oyster Sauce

* Baking Pan

Directions
1. Marinate ingredients for the chicken together for at least 30 minutes in the refrigerator
2. Preheat the Air Fryer to 390 degrees
3. Transfer the marinated chicken to the baking pan. Bake in Air Fryer at for 10 minutes
4. To prepare the sauce, mix all ingredients except the lemon wedges together
5. Pour the sauce mixture over the half-baked chicken. Spread the lemon wedges evenly in the pan and squeeze. The lemon juice and zest will enhance the flavor of the chicken while tenderizing it
6. Continue to cook in the Air Fryer for another 15 minutes, turning the chicken halfway to ensure that each piece is evenly browned
7. Serve over rice or a side of vegetables

LEMONGRASS BEEF

Ingredients
14 Ozs Beef Flank
1 Tsp Sugar
4 Garlic Cloves, finely minced
2 Lemongrass Stalks, finely minced
1 Tbsp Fish Sauce
1 Tbsp Soy Sauce
2 Tbsps Olive Oil

For the Dipping Sauce:
1/2 Red Bird Chili, thinly sliced
1/2 Tbsp Minced Garlic
2 Tbsps Fish Sauce
Juice of 1 Lime
2 Tsps Sugar

Directions
1. Slice the beef flank thinly against the grain
2. In a wide bowl, whisk together sugar, pepper, garlic, lemon grass, fish sauce, and olive oil
3. Add the beef, toss to coat, and refrigerate for at least 2 hours
4. Preheat the Air Fryer to 390 degrees
5. Place the beef into the Air Fryer tray and cook for 6 to 8 minutes or to desired doneness
6. Mix all dipping sauce ingredients together, ensuring that the sugar is well dissolved
7. Serve over rice with the dipping sauce

MARINATED LAMB CHOPS

Ingredients
11 Ozs Lamb Chops
1 Tbsp Sweet Soy Sauce
2 Tsps Minced Garlic
Black Pepper to taste

Directions
1. Mix the sweet soy sauce, garlic and pepper until evenly combined
2. Smear the lamp chops thoroughly with marinade and then leave for one hour
3. Preheat the Air Fryer to 350 degrees
4. When ready, place the lamb chops in the Air Fryer tray and cook for 10 to 12 minutes until tender
5. Serve with a side of potatoes or mash

MEAT LOAF

Ingredients
14 Ozs Ground Beef
4 Mushrooms, sliced
1 Egg, lightly beaten
3 Tbsps Breadcrumbs
2 Ozs Salami, finely chopped
1 Onion, finely chopped
1 Tbsp Fresh Thyme
Black Pepper to taste
1 Tsp Salt
* Oven Safe Dish

Directions
1. Preheat the Air Fryer to 390 degrees
2. Mix the beef in a bowl with the egg, breadcrumbs, salami, onion, thyme, salt and a generous amount of pepper. Knead and mix thoroughly
3. Transfer the beef to the dish and smoothen the top. Press in the mushrooms and coat the top with olive oil
4. Place the dish in the Air Fryer tray and cook for 25 minutes. Roast the meat loaf until nicely brown and done
5. Allow to stand for at least 10 minutes to rest. Serve cut up in wedges

MEXICAN CHICKEN KABOBS

Ingredients
1 Chicken Breast
2 Tbsps Olive Oil
1 Tsp Ground Cumin
2 Tbsps Cilantro, diced
Juice of 1 Lime
Salt and Pepper to taste
1 Zucchini
1 Onion, cut into wedges
1 Bell Pepper
10 Cherry Tomatoes
Cooking Spray
* Bamboo Skewers

Directions
1. Slice the onion into wedges and the bell pepper and zucchini into 1 inch pieces. Cut the chicken breast into small even cubes
2. Combine the salt and pepper, oil, cumin, cilantro, and lime juice in a bowl. Toss in the chicken cubes and then refrigerate for 2 hours
3. Preheat the Air Fryer at 350 degrees
4. Take each skewer and alternate threading of the vegetables and chicken
5. Lightly spray each skewer with oil, and place in the Air Fryer tray
6. Cook for approximately 15 to 18 minutes until meat is well charred

MEXICAN FRIED FISH

Ingredients
2 Basa Fish Fillets
2 Tsps Grated Parmesan Cheese
1 Tsp Red Chili Powder
1/2 Cup Nacho Chips
1/2 Cup Breadcrumbs
2 Tsps Chopped Coriander
Salt and Pepper to taste
2 Tsps Plain Flour
1 Tbsp Lemon Juice
1 Tsp Mustard
2 Eggs

Directions
1. In a bowl, add the eggs, mustard, cheese, salt, red chili powder, flour, lemon juice and mix thoroughly
2. Cut the fish fillets into fingers and marinate in the mixture for 5 minutes
3. Crush the nachos and mix with the breadcrumbs and chopped coriander. Coat the marinated fish in this mixture
4. Preheat the Air Fryer to 340 degrees and fry fish pieces in batches for 10 minutes
5. Serve with tartare or cocktail sauce

MOCHIKO CHICKEN

Ingredients
4 Chicken Breasts
1 Cup White Rice Flour
1/3 Cup Cornstarch
1 Cup Soy Sauce
1 ½ Tbsps Salt
1/3 Cup Sugar
1 Cup Green Onions, chopped
5 Cloves Garlic, minced
1 Tsp Cayenne Pepper
5 Eggs

Directions
1. Combine all ingredients except for the chicken in a bowl. Ensure that it is mixed well
2. Cut the chicken breasts into even strips and add to the mixture. Cover with cling film and allow to marinate overnight in the refrigerator
3. Preheat the Air Fryer to 350 degrees
4. Place marinated chicken strips into the Air Fryer tray and cook for 18 minutes until golden
5. Serve with spicy sauce

MUSHROOM AND PEPPERONI PIZZA

Ingredients
1 Portobello Mushroom Cap
1/2 Tbsp Olive Oil
1 Tbsp Tomato Sauce
1 Tbsp Mozzarella, shredded
4 Slices Pepperoni
1 Pinch Salt
1 Tsp Dried Italian Herbs
1/2 Tsp Red Chili Flakes

Directions
1. Preheat the Air Fryer to 340 degrees
2. Drizzle olive oil on both sides of the Portobello cap, then sprinkle the inside with salt and the Italian seasonings
3. Spread the tomato sauce evenly around the mushroom and then top with cheese
4. Place the mushroom into the Air Fryer and cook for one minute. Remove the cooking tray from the Air Fryer and place the pepperoni slices on top of the Portobello pizza. Cook for an additional 3 to 5 minutes
5. Finish with red pepper flakes

MUSHROOM TARRAGON CHICKEN

Ingredients
2 Chicken Breasts, diced
4 ½ Ozs Mushrooms, sliced
1 ½ Cup Chicken Stock
1/2 Cup Cream
1/2 Tbsp Corn Flour
1 Sprig Fresh Tarragon, finely chopped
1 Shallot, sliced thinly
Salt and Pepper to taste
* Oven Safe Bowl

Directions
1. Preheat the Air Fryer to 350 degrees
2. Add the chicken pieces into the bowl, then place into the Air Fryer to cook for 3 minutes
3. Open the Air Fryer and add the shallots and mushrooms to the bowl. Season with salt and pepper then cook for another 7 minutes
4. Mix the chicken stock, corn flour and the cream evenly. Add to the bowl and cook for another 3 minutes
5. Serve with chopped tarragon on top

MUSTARD CHICKEN

Ingredients
2 lbs Chicken Wings
1 Tbsp Chicken Salt
2 Tbsps Garlic Powder
2 Tbsps Onion Powder
2 Tbsps Black Pepper
3 Tbsps Mustard
3 Cups Plain Flour

Directions
1. Preheat the Air Fryer to 350 degrees
2. Combine the pepper, garlic powder, onion powder and chicken salt in a bowl. Use this mix to season the chicken wings
3. Using a brush, lightly coat the wings with the mustard. Pour the flour onto a shallow plate and roll each coated wing on each side
4. Place the chicken into the Air Fryer and cook in batches for 22 minutes
5. Season to taste with salt and pepper

OAT CRUSTED FISH

Ingredients
4 Cod Fillets
1 Egg, whisked
1/3 Cup Milk
2 Tbsps Plain Flour
2 Cups Quick Cook Oats
Salt and Black Pepper

Directions
1. Preheat the Air Fryer to 350 degrees
2. Combine the egg and milk in a bowl and set aside
3. Take each cod fillet and cover evenly with the flour. Then dip the cod into the egg, and finally cover the cod in oats
4. Place the fish into the Air Fryer and cook in batches for 6 to 8 minutes
5. Season with salt and pepper before serving

ORANGE CHICKEN AND BROWN RICE

Ingredients
2 Chicken Thighs, chopped
1 Tbsp Olive Oil
1 Onion, chopped
3/4 Cup Chicken Broth
1 Cup Brown Rice
Juice and Zest of 1 Orange
Salt and Pepper to taste
2 Tbsps Chopped Fresh Mint
* Baking Dish

Directions
1. Preheat the Air Fryer to 375 degrees
2. Heat the oil in a skillet over medium-high heat. Add the onions and cook, stirring, until just beginning to brown and soft
3. Add the onions, chicken broth, rice, orange juice, zest and salt to the baking dish and stir to combine
4. Toss the chicken with salt and pepper in a medium bowl, then place thighs into the rice mixture. Pour the entire mixture into the baking dish
5. Transfer the baking dish into the Air Fryer and cook for 45 minutes, until most of the liquid has been absorbed. The chicken should be fully cooked and the rice tender. Cook for longer depending on the size of the chicken pieces
6. Sprinkle the mint and desired amount of remaining orange zest over the dish and serve

PARMESAN BREADED PORK CHOPS

Ingredients
4 Pork Chops
1 Egg
1 Tsp Salt
1/4 Tsp Black Pepper
1/3 Cup Parmesan cheese, shredded
1/3 Cup Breadcrumbs
2 Tbsps Plain Flour
2 Tsps Vegetable Oil

Directions
1. Preheat the Air Fryer to 375 degrees
2. Cover the pork chops with the flour evenly
3. Mix the egg, salt and pepper together in a bowl. In another bowl, combine the Parmesan and breadcrumbs
4. Dredge the floured pork chops in the egg mix, then roll in the crumb mixture
5. In a pan, heat the oil and sear each chop until lightly browned. Remove from the heat
6. Place browned chops into the Air Fryer tray and cook for 35 minutes. Allow to rest under foil for 10 minutes before serving

PARMIGIANA SCHNITZEL

Ingredients
1 Crumbed Schnitzel, beef or chicken
3 Tbsps Tomato Based Pasta Sauce
1/4 Cup Grated Parmesan Cheese

Directions
1. Preheat the Air Fryer to 350 degrees
2. Add the schnitzel to the Air Fryer tray and cook for 15 minutes
3. Generously spoon the pasta sauce onto cooked schnitzel, ensuring that all edges are covered
4. Sprinkle with the cheese and replace schnitzel in the Air Fryer for an additional 5 minutes until the meat is cooked through and the cheese is melted

PEANUT SATAY PORK

Ingredients
11 Ozs Pork Fillet, sliced into bite sized strips
4 Cloves Garlic, crushed
1 Tsp Ginger Powder
2 Tsps Chili Paste
2 Tbsps Sweet Soy Sauce (Kecap Manis)
2 Tbsps Vegetable Oil
1 Shallot, finely chopped
1 Tsp Ground Coriander
3/4 Cup Coconut Milk
1/3 Cup Peanuts, ground

Directions
1. Mix half of the garlic in a dish with the ginger, a tablespoon of sweet soy sauce, and a tablespoon of the oil. Combine the meat into the mixture and leave to marinate for 15 minutes
2. Preheat the Air Fryer to 390 degrees
3. Place the marinated meat into the Air Fryer. Set the timer to 12 minutes and roast the meat until brown and done. Turn once while roasting
4. In the meantime, make the peanut sauce by heating the remaining tablespoon of oil in a saucepan and gently sauté the shallot with the garlic. Add the coriander and fry until fragrant
5. Mix the coconut milk and the peanuts with the chili paste and remaining soy sauce with the shallot mixture and gently boil for 5 minutes, while stirring
6. Drizzle over the cooked meat and serve with rice

PORK CUTLET ROLLS

Ingredients
4 Pork Cutlets
4 Sundried Tomatoes in oil
2 Tbsps Parsley, finely chopped
1 Green Onion, finely chopped
Black Pepper to taste
2 Tsps Paprika
1/2 Tbsp Olive Oil
* String for Rolled Meat

Directions
1. Preheat the Air Fryer to 390 degrees
2. Finely chop the tomatoes and mix with the parsley and green onion. Add salt and pepper to taste
3. Spread out the cutlets and coat them with the tomato mixture. Roll up the cutlets and secure intact with the string
4. Rub the rolls with salt, pepper, and paprika powder and thinly coat them with olive oil
5. Put the cutlet rolls in the Air Fryer tray and cook for 15 minutes. Roast until nicely brown and done
6. Serve with tomato sauce

PORK TENDERS WITH BELL PEPPERS

Ingredients
11 Ozs Pork Tenderloin
1 Bell Pepper, in thin strips
1 Red Onion, sliced
2 Tsps Provencal Herbs
Black Pepper to taste
1 Tbsp Olive Oil
1/2 Tbsp Mustard
* Round Oven Dish

Directions
1. Preheat the Air Fryer to 390 degrees
2. In the oven dish, mix the bell pepper strips with the onion, herbs, and some salt and pepper to taste. Add half a tablespoon of olive oil to the mixture
3. Cut the pork tenderloin into four pieces and rub with salt, pepper and mustard. Thinly coat the pieces with remaining olive oil and place them upright in the oven dish on top of the pepper mixture
4. Place the bowl into the Air Fryer. Set the timer to 15 minutes and roast the meat and the vegetables
5. Turn the meat and mix the peppers halfway through
6. Serve with a fresh salad

POTATO CRUSTED BEEF TENDERS

Ingredients
3 lbs Beef Tenderloin, cut into 2 pieces
8 Potatoes, peeled and quartered
1 Cup Panko Breadcrumbs
2 Tbsps Minced Garlic
1 Tbsp Minced Fresh Thyme
1 ½ Cups Heavy Cream
1 ½ Cups Flour
Salt and Black Pepper
3 Ozs Butter
5 Eggs

Directions
1. Preheat the Air Fryer to 350 degrees
2. In a saucepan, add potatoes and fill with salted cold water. Slowly boil potatoes for 35 minutes until potatoes come cleanly off of a knife
3. In another hot saucepan coated with oil, caramelize garlic then add thyme and cream. Reduce cream by 30 percent
4. In a mixing bowl, add hot potatoes and garlic cream. Mix together until smooth. Add butter, salt and pepper and check for seasoning. Allow to cool
5. Whisk together 3 eggs and one cup of flour until smooth. Mix with the cool mash
6. Season both pieces of beef well with salt and pepper. Coat with 1/2-inch of potato puree. Dredge the coated beef in remaining flour, then 2 beaten eggs, then panko
7. Place beef into the Air Fryer tray and cook until golden brown for 8 minutes for a medium rare result. Allow to rest for 5 minutes before slicing

PRAWN PASTED CHICKEN

Ingredients
10 Ozs Chicken Wings
1 Cup Corn Flour

For the Marinade:
1 Tbsp Shrimp Paste
3/4 Tsp Sugar
1 Tsp Sesame Oil
1 Tsp Minced Ginger
1/2 Tsp Shaoxing Wine

Directions
1. Combine the marinade ingredients in a bowl until it forms a paste. Coat the wings in the sauce and cover with cling film. Allow to marinate overnight in the refrigerator
2. When the chicken is ready, coat the wings evenly with corn flour
3. Heat the Air Fryer to 350 degrees
4. Place the coated chicken wings in the Air Fryer and cook for 12 minutes. Rotate the chicken pieces and continue cooking for another 10 minutes until crispy
5. Serve with soy sauce

RATATOUILLE

Ingredients
7 Ozs Courgette
1 Yellow Bell Pepper
2 Tomatoes
1 Onion
1 Clove Garlic, minced
2 Tsps Dried Provencal Herbs
Salt and Black Pepper to taste
1 Tsp Olive Oil
* Small Round Baking Dish

Directions
1. Preheat the Air Fryer to 390 degrees
2. Cut the courgette, bell pepper, tomatoes, and onion into 2cm cubes
3. Mix the vegetables in the baking dish with the garlic, herbs, olive oil, and some salt and pepper to taste
4. Put the dish into the Air Fryer for 15 minutes and cook the ratatouille. Stir the vegetables once when cooking
5. Serve as a side with meat

ROASTED CORNISH GAME HEN

Ingredients
1 Cornish Hen
1/2 Cup Olive Oil
1/4 Tsp Red Pepper Flakes
1 Tsp Chopped Thyme
1 Tsp Chopped Rosemary
1/4 Tsp Salt
1/4 Tsp Sugar
Zest of 1 Lemon

Directions
1. Place the whole Cornish hen on a cutting board. Using a boning knife, set the hen upright with the back facing you. Start from the top of the back bone to the bottom of the back bone. Make two cuts and remove the back bone
2. Once the back bone is removed, split the hen lengthwise cutting through the breastplate. You should have two whole halves of Cornish hen set aside
3. In a mixing bowl, combine all ingredients for the marinade. Add the hen halves to the mixture and refrigerate overnight
4. Preheat the Air Fryer to 375 degrees
5. Cook the hen in the Air Fryer for 18 to 20 minutes depending on the size of the chicken
6. Allow meat to rest for 10 minutes before serving

ROASTED MACADAMIA LAMB

Ingredients
1.7 lbs Rack of Lamb
2 Garlic Cloves, minced
1 Tbsp Olive Oil
Salt and Pepper to taste
1/2 Cup Unsalted Macadamias
1 Tbsp Breadcrumbs
1 Tbsp Rosemary, diced
1 Egg

Directions
1. Combine the olive oil and garlic, then brush over the lamb to coat evenly
2. Heat the Air Fryer to 250 degrees
3. Pulse the nuts in a food processor until it forms a crumbly texture. Mix in the rosemary and breadcrumbs then transfer to a bowl
4. Beat the egg and then brush onto the lamb rack, coating well. Season with salt and pepper
5. Roll the lamb into the breadcrumb mixture, ensuring that you have used enough egg for it to adhere
6. Place the lamb in the Air Fryer tray and cook for 20 minutes. Increase the temperature to 390 degrees and roast for a further 8 minutes
7. Allow the lamb to rest before serving

SALMON PATTIES

Ingredients
15 Oz Canned Salmon, drained and liquid reserved
1/3 Cup Onion, chopped
1/2 Cup All Purpose Flour
1 ½ Tsps Baking Powder
1/4 Cup Cornmeal
1 Egg

Directions
1. Mix salmon, onion, and egg together in a bowl, then stir in flour
2. Stir baking powder and 2 tablespoons of reserved salmon liquid together in a separate bowl. Stir into salmon mixture until mixture holds together when shaped. Shape the mixture into small patties
3. Preheat the Air Fryer to 350 degrees
4. Spread cornmeal into a shallow bowl and press onto patties until evenly coated on both sides
5. Place patties into the Air Fryer tray and cook for 10 minutes until golden brown
6. Serve in a hamburger bun or with a side salad

SALMON QUICHE

Ingredients
5 Ozs Salmon Fillet
1/2 Tbsp Lemon Juice
1/2 Cup Flour
1/4 Cup Butter, melted
2 Eggs and 1 Egg Yolk
3 Tbsps Whipped Cream
2 Tsps Mustard
Black Pepper to taste
Salt and Pepper
* Quiche Pan

Directions
1. Clean and cut the salmon into small cubes
2. Heat the Air Fryer to 375 degrees
3. Pour the lemon juice over the salmon cubes and allow to marinate for an hour
4. Combine a tablespoon of water with the butter, flour and yolk in a large bowl. Using your hands, knead the mixture until smooth
5. On a clean surface, use a rolling pin to form a circle of dough. Place this into the quiche pan, using your fingers to adhere the pastry to the edges
6. Whisk the cream, mustard and eggs together. Season with salt and pepper. Add the marinated salmon into the bowl and combine
7. Pour the content of the bowl into the dough lined quiche pan
8. Put the pan in the Air Fryer tray and cook for 25 minutes until browned and crispy

SALMON RISSOLES

Ingredients
2 x 14 Oz Cans of Salmon, drained
2 Cups Cornflakes, crushed
1 Onion, diced
2 Eggs, beaten
1 Tsp Dried Basil
1 Tsp Dried Oregano
1 Tsp Dried Thyme
2 Tbsps All Purpose Flour

Directions
1. In a medium bowl, mix salmon, crushed cornflakes, and onion. Blend in the eggs. Season with basil, oregano, and thyme
2. Form the mixture into 1 inch balls. Roll in flour to lightly coat
3. Preheat the Air Fryer to 350 degrees
4. In batches, fry the salmon balls for about 12 minutes until golden brown

SALMON WITH DILL SAUCE

Ingredients
12 Ozs Salmon Fillet
2 Tsps Olive Oil

For the Sauce:
1/2 Cup Greek Yogurt
1/2 Cup Sour Cream
Pinch of Salt
2 Tbsps Dill, diced

Directions
1. Heat the Air Fryer to 350 degrees
2. Cut the salmon into two equal pieces. Coat each portion in the oil
3. Place the salmon fillets in the Air Fryer and cook for 15 minutes
4. Whilst the salmon is cooking, combine all ingredients for the sauce in a bowl and mix well
5. Transfer the salmon onto a serving platter and pour the sauce over the top

SNAPPER WITH ASIAN DRESSING

Ingredients
1 Whole Small Snapper, scaled and gutted
2 Cucumbers
1 Red Capsicum, cut into strips
1/2 Cup Fresh Coriander
1/2 Cup Fresh Mint
Salt and Black Pepper to taste

For the Asian-Style Dressing:
2 Tbsps Tamarind Pulp
1/2 Cup Warm Water
1 Tbsp Peanut Oil
4 Garlic Cloves, chopped
1 Fresh Red Birdseye Chili, deseeded and chopped
2 Tbsps Palm Sugar
2 Tsps Fish Sauce

Directions
1. Wash the fish and use paper towel to dry both inside and out thoroughly
2. To make the dressing, place the tamarind pulp and water in a small bowl. Set aside for 2 minutes or until tamarind softens. Rub tamarind with your fingers to remove the pulp from the seeds and fiber. Strain liquid into a small bowl
3. Heat the oil in a saucepan over medium heat. Add the garlic and chili, and cook, stirring, for one minute. Remove from the heat. Add the tamarind liquid, palm sugar and fish sauce. Stir to combine
4. Run a vegetable peeler down the length of the cucumbers to form long ribbons. Place in a medium bowl with the capsicum, coriander, mint and half of the dressing. Toss gently to combine
5. Rub salt and pepper over surface of fish. Use a sharp knife to cut 3 slashes and 1cm deep in the thickest part of the flesh on both sides of fish

6. Preheat the Air Fryer to 375 degrees
7. Place the snapper into the Air Fryer tray and cook for 13 minutes or until golden and the flesh flakes easily
8. To serve, arrange the cucumber and capsicum salad on a serving platter. Carefully place the fried fish on top of the salad. Drizzle with the remaining dressing and serve immediately

SOBA SALMON NOODLES

Ingredients
1 Salmon Fillet
1 Tbsp Teriyaki Marinade
3 ½ Ozs Soba Noodles, cooked and drained
10 Ozs Firm Tofu
7 Ozs Mixed Salad
1 Cup Broccoli
Olive Oil
Salt and Pepper to taste

Directions
1. Season the salmon with salt and pepper to taste, then coat with the teriyaki marinate. Set aside for 15 minutes
2. Preheat the Air Fryer at 350 degrees, then cook the salmon for 8 minutes
3. Whilst the Air Fryer is cooking the salmon, start slicing the tofu into small cubes
4. Next, slice the broccoli into smaller chunks. Drizzle with olive oil
5. Once the salmon is cooked, put the broccoli and tofu into the Air Fryer tray for 8 minutes
6. Plate the salmon and broccoli tofu mixture over the soba noodles. Add the mixed salad to the side and serve

SPICY BEEF

Ingredients
1 lb Beef Fillet, cubed
2 Tbsps Sweet Apple Cider
6 Ozs Tomato Paste
1 Tbsp Tabasco Sauce
1 Tsp Cocoa

Directions
1. Preheat the Air Fryer to 390 degrees
2. In a small bowl, mix all ingredients together and rub the beef thoroughly with this mixture
3. Allow to marinate for an hour
4. Please marinated beef into the Air Fryer tray and cook for 12 minutes, tossing it through at the midpoint to ensure it is even
5. Serve with rice or side vegetables

SPINACH AND FETA PIE

Ingredients
2 Cups Chopped Spinach
1/2 Cup Feta Cheese, crumbled
2 Tbsps Oil
3 Cloves Garlic, diced
1 Onion, diced
1 Bunch Swiss Chard, chopped
1/2 Cup Rice
1 Egg
3 Tbsps Dill, chopped
3 Tbsps Pine Nuts
1 Tsp Lemon Zest
12 Sheets Phyllo Pastry
1/2 Cup Butter, melted
Salt to taste

Directions
1. Heat the Air Fryer to 390 degrees
2. In a pan, heat the oil and sauté the garlic and onion until soft
3. Add the rice, a cup of water and season with salt. Place a lid over the pan and leave to simmer for 10 minutes. Once the rice is almost cooked, toss the chard and spinach into the pan for another minute. Place the mixture in a bowl and allow to cool
4. Once cooled, add the feta, egg, dill, pine nuts and lemon zest to the filling. Stir to combine well
5. On a clean surface, lay out 4 sheets of pastry to form the pie base. Brush the surface of each sheet with the melted butter and lay the next sheet over it cross-wise
6. Spoon the filling into the center of the base and spread to even thickness. Press the edges of the pastry upwards to form a circle
7. Use the remaining pastry sheets to cover the top of the pie to enclose the filling. Continue to use butter to brush

and adhere each layer. Repeat the process to form a round freestanding pie

8. Place the pie into the Air Fryer and cook for 35 or more minutes. The pastry should be crisp and lightly brown when ready

9. Serve hot with a side salad

SPINACH QUICHE

Ingredients
7 Ozs Spinach
2/3 Cup Flour
1/3 Cup Butter
2 Tbsps Milk
Salt and Pepper to taste
1 Onion, chopped
1 Tbsp Olive Oil
1/2 Cup Cottage Cheese
1 Egg
* 4 Small Ramekins

Directions
1. Place the flour, butter, and milk into a food processor with a pinch of salt and blend until it forms a dough. Place onto a worktop and knead with your hands until smooth. Cover with cling wrap and allow to rest in the refrigerator for 15 minutes
2. Heat the oil in a pan and add the onion. Cook until translucent, then add the spinach and fry for 1 to 2 minutes until wilted
3. In a bowl, whisk the egg, stir in the cottage cheese, and add the cooked spinach mixture
4. Divide the rested dough into 4 equal parts. Roll each part into a circle, large enough to cover the bottom of the ramekin. Line the ramekins with the dough. Fill each mold with the spinach filling
5. Preheat the Air Fryer to 350 degrees
6. Place the quiches into the Air Fryer tray and cook for 15 minutes
7. Serve with a side salad

SPINACH STUFFED CHICKEN BREAST

Ingredients
4 Chicken Breasts
4 Slices Bacon
1/2 Cup Mayonnaise
10 Ozs Spinach, chopped
1/2 Cup Feta Cheese
3 Cloves Garlic, minced

Directions
1. Preheat the Air Fryer at 350 degrees
2. Combine the feta, spinach, mayonnaise and garlic in a bowl
3. Make a lengthwise cut in the center of each chicken breast. Fill the cavity with the feta mixture until almost full
4. Taking a piece of bacon, wrap around each breast to enclose the filling. Use a toothpick to secure this in place. Repeat with all chicken breasts
5. Place into the Air Fryer and bake for 40 minutes until the chicken is cooked through
6. Serve with a side of vegetables

STICKY BARBEQUE PORK RIBS

Ingredients
6 Pork Loin Chops
1 Tsp Balsamic Vinegar
2 Tbsps Soy Sauce
2 Tbsps Honey
1 Clove Minced Garlic
1/2 Tsp Grated Ginger
Black Pepper to taste

Directions
1. Use a meat tenderizer to tenderize the chops, then season with black pepper
2. To prepare the marinade, pour the balsamic vinegar, soy sauce, ginger, garlic and honey into a bowl and mix well
3. Combine the pork chops with the mixture and leave it to marinate for 2 hours or overnight
4. Preheat the Air Fryer at 350 degrees
5. Place the chops into the Air Fryer tray and cook for 9 minutes on each side. Chops are done when they are golden brown
6. To serve, cut the meat into strips or plate whole as chops

SWEET AND SOUR CHICKEN

Ingredients
3 Chicken Breasts, cubed
1/2 Cup Flour
1/2 Cup Cornstarch
2 Red Peppers, sliced
1 Onion, chopped
2 Carrots, julienned
3/4 Cup Sugar
2 Tbsps Cornstarch
1/3 Cup Vinegar
2/3 Cup Water
1/4 cup Soy sauce
1 Tbsp Ketchup

Directions
1. Preheat the Air Fryer to 375 degrees
2. Combine the flour, cornstarch and chicken in an air tight container and shake to combine
3. Remove chicken from the container and shake off any excess flour
4. Add chicken to the Air Fryer tray and cook for 20 minutes
5. In a saucepan, whisk together sugar, water, vinegar, soy sauce and ketchup. Bring to a boil over medium heat, reduce the heat then simmer for 2 minutes
6. After cooking the chicken for 20 minutes, add the vegetables and sauce mixture to the Air Fryer and cook for another 5 minutes
7. Serve over hot rice

TANDOORI CHICKEN

Ingredients
4 Chicken Legs

For the First Marinade:
3 Tsps Ginger Paste
3 Tsps Minced Garlic
3 Tbsps Lemon Juice

For the Second Marinade:
2 Tbsps Tandoori Masala Powder
1 Tsp Roasted Cumin
1 Tsp Garam Masala
2 Tsps Ground Coriander
2 Tsps Red Chili Powder
1 Tsp Turmeric
4 Tbsps Hung Curd
2 Tsps Kasuri Methi
1 Tsp Black pepper

Directions
1. Wash the chicken and make slits in them using a sharp knife
2. Add chicken in a bowl along with the ingredients for the first marinade. Mix well and set aside for 20 minutes
3. Combine ingredients for the second marinade and pour mixture over the chicken. Cover the bowl and refrigerate overnight
4. Preheat the Air Fryer to 390 degrees
5. Place the chicken into the tray and cook for 20 minutes until browned
6. Serve with yogurt and rice

TERIYAKI CHICKEN

Ingredients
6 Skinless Chicken Thighs
1 Tbsp Cornstarch
1 Tbsp Cold Water
1/2 Cup Sugar
1/2 Cup Soy Sauce
1/4 Cup Cider Vinegar
1 Clove Garlic, minced
1/2 Tsp Ground Ginger
1/4 Tsp Ground Black Pepper
* Baking Dish

Directions
1. In a small saucepan over low heat, combine the cornstarch, water, sugar, soy sauce, vinegar, garlic, ginger and black pepper. Let simmer, stirring frequently, until the sauce thickens
2. Preheat the Air Fryer at 400 degrees
3. Place chicken pieces into the baking dish and brush again with the marinade
4. Place the dish into the Air Fryer tray and cook for 30 minutes. Turn pieces over, and bake for another 15 minutes, until no longer pink and juices run clear
5. Serve on hot rice

THAI BASIL CHICKEN

Ingredients
4 Chicken Breasts
1 Onion
2 Bell Peppers
2 Hot Peppers
1 Tbsp Olive Oil
3 Tbsps Fish Sauce
2 Tbsps Oyster Sauce
3 Tbsps Sweet Chili Sauce
1 Tbsp Soy Sauce
1 Quart Chicken Broth
1 Tbsp Garlic Powder
1 Tbsp Chili Powder
1 Cup Thai Basil

Directions
1. Wash the breasts and boil them in the chicken broth for 10 minutes, then lower to simmer for another 10 minutes until tender. Take them out of the broth and allow to cool
2. Using two forks, tear the chicken into shreds. Toss the shreds with the garlic powder, chili powder, and salt and pepper to taste
3. Preheat the Air Fryer to 390 degrees and cook the chicken shreds for 20 minutes, at which point they will get dark brown and crispy. They will soften up as they absorb the juices from cooking with the veggies
4. While the chicken is cooking, cut the onions and peppers into thin slices. Add the olive oil to a wok and heat for a minute on medium high heat. Toss in all the veggies and sauté for 5 minutes
5. Add in the fish sauce, oyster sauce, soy sauce, sweet chili sauce, and stir well for 1 minute. Add the chicken and basil leaves and stir until the leaves have wilted
6. Serve over jasmine rice

THAI FISH CAKES WITH MANGO RELISH

Ingredients
1 lb White Fish Fillets
3 Tbsps Ground Coconut
1 Ripened Mango
1 ½ Tsps Chili Paste
2 Tbsps Fresh Parsley
1 Green Onion
1 Lime
1 Tsp Salt
1 Egg

Directions
1. To make the relish, peel and dice the mango into cubes. Combine with a half teaspoon of chili paste, a tablespoon of parsley, and the zest and juice of half a lime
2. In a food processor, pulse the fish until it forms a smooth texture. Place into a bowl and add the salt, egg, chopped green onion, parsley, two tablespoons of the coconut, and the remainder of the chili paste and lime zest and juice. Combine well
3. Portion the mixture into 10 equal balls and flatten them into small patties. Pour the reserved tablespoon of coconut onto a dish and roll the patties over to coat
4. Preheat the Air Fryer to 390 degrees
5. Place the fish cakes into the Air Fryer and cook for 8 minutes. They should be crisp and lightly browned when ready
6. Serve hot with mango relish

THAI FRIED CHICKEN

Ingredients
12 Chicken Drumsticks
1/2 Cup Honey Mustard
1/2 Cup Sweet Chili Sauce
4 Cups Panko Breadcrumbs
2 Eggs, beaten
Sea Salt to taste

Directions
1. Whisk together the honey mustard, chili sauce, eggs, and sea salt in a bowl to form a marinade
2. Place the chicken drumsticks in a large, sealable plastic bag. Pour the marinade over the chicken and seal the bag. Allow to chill in refrigerator at least 4 hours
3. Preheat the Air Fryer to 350 degrees
4. Place the breadcrumbs onto a plate. Dredge the marinated chicken in the breadcrumbs to coat
5. Place the breaded chicken into the Air Fryer in batches and cook for 20 minutes until golden brown, turning once for evenness

TOMATO AND CHICKEN PASTA

Ingredients
3 Chicken Breasts
14 Ozs Canned Italian Chopped Tomatoes
1 Tsp Dried Basil
1/2 Tsp Mixed Herbs
1 Tsp Lemon Juice
1 Tsp Pesto
3 Serves of Penne Pasta
Salt and Pepper to taste
1/2 Onion, diced
2 Bacon Rashers, diced

Directions
1. Preheat the Air Fryer to 350 degrees
2. Season chicken with salt, pepper and lemon juice, add to Air Fryer and cook for 10 minutes
3. Add the onion, herbs, tomatoes, basil and bacon and cook for a further 10 minutes
4. Once the mixture is mixed together and fragrant, add the pesto and cook for 7 minutes
5. Serve over cooked pasta with some grated cheese

TURKEY AND MUSHROOM PATTIES

Ingredients
1 lb Ground Turkey
6 Mushrooms, chopped
1 Tbsp Soy Sauce
1 Tsp Garlic Powder
1 Tsp Onion Powder
1/2 Tsp Salt
1/2 Tsp Black Pepper

Directions
1. In a small bowl, mix together all the ingredients until well combined
2. Portion the mixture into 6 even balls and flatten to form patties
3. Preheat the Air Fryer to 375 degrees
4. Place patties in the Air Fryer tray and cook for 13 minutes
5. Serve hot on a hamburger bun

TURKEY CHEESEBURGER MEATLOAF

Ingredients
8 Slices Turkey Bacon
1 lb Ground Turkey
1 Cup Cheddar Cheese, grated
1/2 Onion, diced
1 Cup Breadcrumbs
2 Tbsps Worcestershire Sauce
2 Tsps Garlic Powder
1/4 Tsp Pepper
1/4 Cup Ketchup
2 Tbsps Mustard
1 ½ Tbsps Sugar
1 Tsp Vegetable Oil
1 Egg
* Baking Loaf Tray

Directions
1. Preheat the Air Fryer at 350 degrees
2. In a pan over a medium flame, heat the oil and cook the turkey bacon until it is crispy enough to crumble
3. In a large bowl, combine the bacon, ground turkey, cheddar, egg, onion, crumbs, Worcestershire sauce, garlic powder, and pepper
4. Place the mixture into the baking dish and form into a loaf shape
5. Stir the ketchup, mustard, and sugar so that all components dissolve together. Pour over the loaf to cover
6. Place the baking tray into the Air Fryer and cook for 45 minutes or more. The loaf is ready when it is no longer pink in the center

TURKEY QUINOA MEATLOAF

Ingredients
1 lb Ground Turkey
1/4 Cup Quinoa
1/2 Cup Water
1 Tsp Olive Oil
1 Onion, chopped
1 Clove Garlic, chopped
1 Tbsp Tomato Paste
1 Tbsp Hot Pepper Sauce
2 Tbsps Worcestershire Sauce
1 Egg
1 ½ Tsps Salt
1 Tsp Pepper
* Baking Loaf Tray

Directions
1. Preheat Air Fryer at 350 degrees
2. Cook quinoa according to package instructions
3. Heat the olive oil in a skillet over medium heat. Stir in the onion and cook until translucent. Add the garlic and cook for another minute
4. Stir the turkey, cooked quinoa, onions and garlic mixture, tomato paste, hot sauce, egg, salt, pepper, and Worcestershire in a large bowl until well combined
5. Pour the mixture into the baking tray and shape into a loaf. Place the baking tray into the Air Fryer and cook for 45 minutes or until the loaf is no longer pink in the middle

VEAL KEBAB

Ingredients
1 lb Veal Tenderloin
1 Tbsp Lemon Juice
1 Tsp Red Chili Pepper
2 Carrots
1 Cup Tomato Sauce
1 Clove Garlic
6 Shallots
2 Tsps Olive Oil

Directions
1. Cut the veal tenderloin into cubes and marinate in lemon juice, tomato sauce and red chili powder
2. Preheat the Air Fryer at 390 degrees
3. Finely slice the garlic, shallots and carrots and cook for 10 minutes in the Air Fryer
4. Then add the marinated veal and cook for another 12 minutes or until the meat is of desired tenderness
5. Serve hot with a side salad or vegetables

VEAL SAFFRON RISOTTO

Ingredients
7 Ozs Veal Fillet, sliced
2 Slices Smoked Bacon, diced
2 Slices Ham, diced
1 Pinch Saffron
3 ½ Ozs Tomatoes, diced
2 Cups Chicken Stock
1 ½ Cups Arborio Risotto Rice
1 Clove Garlic, finely chopped
1/2 Tsp Dried Thyme
1 Onion, chopped
Salt and Pepper to taste

Directions
1. Preheat the Air Fryer to 350 degrees
2. Dice the bacon and allow to fry in its own fat for 5 minutes in the Air Fryer. Remove as soon as it starts to color
3. Fry the chopped onions in the bacon fat, add the rice and brown for 2 minutes
4. Add the tomatoes and the garlic. Pour in the chicken stock and add the thyme and saffron. Mix and cook for 15 minutes
5. When the rice begins to increase in volume, add the veal, ham and the bacon. Stir, adjust the seasoning and cook for about 10 additional minutes. Leave to stand for 3 minutes before serving

VENISON BACKSTRAP

Ingredients
2 lbs Venison Backstrap
2 Tbsps Hot Pepper Sauce
3 Cups All Purpose Flour
1 Tbsp Black Pepper
2 ½ Cups Milk
2 Tbsps Salt
2 Eggs

Directions
1. Cut the venison into 1/4 inch thick slices and place into a shallow bowl. Pour 2 cups of the milk and the hot sauce. Stir to coat, then cover and marinate for 1 hour
2. Preheat the Air Fryer to 340 degrees
3. In a shallow bowl, whisk together the eggs and remaining half cup of milk. In a separate bowl, stir together the flour, salt and pepper
4. Dip the venison slices into the flour, then into the egg and milk mix, then back into the flour. Shake off excess flour
5. Fry strips in the Air Fryer until lightly browned on each side, about 6 minutes

ZUCCHINI AND PEPPER RISOTTO

Ingredients
2 Tsps Vegetable Stock Powder
2 Cups Water
14 Ozs Canned Tomato Purée
3 Red Capsicums
1 Zucchini
1 Cup Arborio Risotto Rice
1 Onion, diced
4 Garlic Cloves, minced

Directions
1. Cut the zucchini and capsicum into slices
2. Preheat the Air Fryer to 350 degrees
3. Put the onion and garlic into the tray and cook for 5 minutes
4. Combine vegetable stock with 1½ cups of water and add to dish along with the tomato purée and rice. Cook for 10 minutes
5. Add zucchini and capsicum and the remaining half cup of water. Cook for approximately 25 minutes. Stir occasionally through cooking as the rice needs to be distributed evenly
6. Serve with coriander and grated cheese on top

DESSERTS AND SWEETS

APPLE PASTRY DUMPLINGS

Ingredients
2 Small Apples
2 Tbsps Sultanas
1 Tbsp Brown Sugar
2 Sheets Puff Pastry
2 Tbsps Butter, melted

Directions
1. Preheat the Air Fryer to 350 degrees
2. Core and peel the apples. Mix the sultanas and the brown sugar
3. Place each apple on one of the puff pastry sheets then fill the core with the sultanas and sugar. Fold the pastry around the apple so it is fully covered
4. Brush the dough with the melted butter
5. Place into the Air Fryer tray lined with foil and set the timer to 25 minutes
6. Bake the apple dumplings until golden brown and the apples are soft

BERRY PANCAKE TOPPING

Ingredients
1 ½ Cups Quartered Strawberries
1/2 Cup Blueberries
2 Tbsps Sugar
1 Tbsp Orange Juice
Whipped Cream
Wholegrain Pancakes

Directions
1. Preheat Air Fryer to 350 degrees
2. Cook wholegrain pancakes according to package instructions
3. Rinse the berries and place them into the Air Fryer tray
4. Dissolve the sugar into the orange juice and pour on top of the berries
5. Cook for 8 minutes until topping is thick and slightly caramelized
6. Spoon the berry sauce over each serving of pancakes. Top with whipped cream and garnish with a sliced strawberry

BAKED ALASKAS

Ingredients
4 Egg Whites
1/4 Tsp Salt
1/2 Tsp Cream of Tartar
1/4 Tsp Vanilla Essence
1/4 Cup Icing Sugar
6 Pre-made Shortcake Shells
1 lb Ice Cream, well frozen

Directions
1. Preheat the Air Fryer to 420 degrees
2. Beat egg whites until soft and foamy. Add salt, cream of tartar and vanilla, gradually beating in sugar until stiff, shiny peaks form
3. Fill the center of each shortcake shell with ice cream. Cover each with a layer of meringue, using a spatula
4. Place Alaskas into the Air Fryer and bake for 4 minutes

BANANA AND RHUBARB SLICE

Ingredients
9 Ozs Rhubarb
2 Bananas
1 Cup Sugar
1/4 Tsp Salt
2 Tbsps Butter
* Baking Dish

Directions
1. Preheat the Air Fryer to 375 degrees
2. Wash and cut the rhubarb in 2 inch pieces. Peel and slice the bananas lengthwise
3. Grease the baking dish and alternate layers of rhubarb and banana, ending with rhubarb
4. Combine the sugar and salt and sprinkle this over the top layer. Crumb the butter over the slice
5. Place into the Air Fryer and bake for 40 minutes or until syrup thickens
6. Slices can be served hot or cold

BANANA CAKE

Ingredients
1/4 Cup Butter
1/3 Cup Brown Sugar
Cooking Spray
1 Banana, mashed
2 Tbsps Honey
1 Cup Self Raising Flour
1/2 Tsp Cinnamon
Salt to taste
1 Egg
* Small Ring Cake Tin

Directions
1. Preheat the Air Fryer to 320 degrees
2. Spray the cake tin with the cooking spray
3. In a bowl, beat the butter with the sugar until creamy. Add the egg, banana and honey then whisk into the butter mixture until smooth
4. Sift in the flour, cinnamon and salt then mix to make the cake batter
5. Transfer the batter to the cake tin and use a spatula to level the surface. Put the cake tin in the Air Fryer tray
6. Set the timer to 30 minutes and bake the cake until a toothpick inserted in the center of the cake comes out cleanly

BANANAS IN COCONUT BATTER

Ingredients
8 Bananas
1/2 Cup Rice Flour
1/2 Cup Wheat Flour
1 Tsp Baking Soda
1 Cup Water
1/2 Cup Coconut Milk
1/2 Tsp Salt
3 Tbsps Sesame Seeds
3 Tbsps Sugar
4 Tbsps Desiccated Coconut
Icing Sugar

Directions
1. Peel and slice bananas into two halves
2. Combine all the other ingredients into a large mixing bowl and stir until well combined
3. Preheat the Air Fryer to 390 degrees
4. Dip the banana pieces into the batter and then place into the Air Fryer tray. Fry for 6 minutes until the batter is cooked and golden
5. Dust with icing sugar before serving

BLUEBERRY MUFFINS

Ingredients
1 Cup Blueberries
1 ½ Cups Flour
1/2 Cup Sugar
1/2 Tsp Salt
2 Tsps Baking Powder
1/3 Cup Vegetable Oil
3/4 Cup Yoghurt
2 Tsps Vanilla Extract
1 Egg
* 5 Silicon Muffin Cups

Directions
1. Combine flour, sugar, salt, and baking powder in a large bowl. Whisk well to ensure even consistency
2. In a separate cup, mix the oil, egg, yoghurt and vanilla extract together
3. Add wet to dry ingredients by combining lightly
4. Using a spoon, gently fold in the blueberries being careful not to rupture
5. Pour batter mixture into each muffin cup until 3/4 full. Sprinkle some sugar on top of each muffin
6. Preheat the Air Fryer at 350 degrees
7. Insert muffin cups into the Air Fryer tray and cook for 12 minutes. Use a toothpick to check if they are cooked and adjust as required

BUTTER CAKE

Ingredients
1/2 Cup Butter
1/2 Cup Sugar
1 Egg
1 Cup Flour
1/2 Cup Milk
1 Tsp Icing Sugar
Salt to taste
Cooking Spray
* Small Ring Cake Tin

Directions
1. Preheat the Air Fryer to 350 degrees
2. Spray the cake tin with the cooking spray
3. In a bowl, beat the butter with the sugar until creamy. Add the egg then whisk into the butter mixture until smooth and fluffy
4. Sift in the flour and salt, then mix thoroughly with the milk to create the cake batter
5. Transfer the batter to the cake tin and use the back of a spoon to level the surface. Put the cake tin in the Air Fryer tray
6. Set the timer to 15 minutes and bake the cake until a toothpick inserted in the center of the cake comes out cleanly
7. Turn cake out of cake tin and allow to cool

BUTTER COOKIES

Ingredients
5 Ozs Butter, softened
2 Ozs Sugar
1/2 Cup Cornflour
1/3 Cup All Purpose Flour
1 Tsp Vanilla Extract

Directions:
1. In a mixing bowl, beat the butter, vanilla extract and icing sugar until light and fluffy
2. Add the cornflour and all purpose flour into the butter mixture. Keep mixing until it forms a soft dough. Cover and allow to rest in the refrigerator for 30 minutes
3. Preheat the Air Fryer to 320 degrees
4. Roll dough into small balls and arrange them on the Air Fryer tray. Use a spoon to press lightly on the small round dough
5. Bake the cookies for 13 minutes until desired consistency is achieved

CHERRY CLAFOUTIS

Ingredients
7 Ozs Cherries
1 Egg
2 Tsps Butter
1/4 Cup Flour
2 Tbsps Vodka
2 Tbsps Sugar
1/2 Cup Sour Cream
1 Tsp Icing Sugar
* Cake Pan

Directions
1. Pit the cherries and mix them in a bowl with the vodka
2. Preheat the Air Fryer to 350 degrees
3. In another bowl, mix the flour with the sugar, salt, egg and sour cream until the dough is smooth and thick
4. Butter the cake pan and spoon the batter in. Place the cherries evenly over the top of the batter and place the remaining butter in small chunks evenly on top
5. Put the cake pan in the Air Fryer tray and cook for 25 minutes. Bake the clafoutis until it is golden brown and done
6. Immediately after baking, dust the clafoutis with plenty of powdered sugar
7. Serve the lukewarm in slices

CHOCOLATE BROWNIES

Ingredients
5 Ozs Pecan Nuts, chopped
4 Ozs Dark Chocolate
4 Ozs White Chocolate
2 Tbsps Vanilla Extract
1/2 Cup Flour
7 Ozs Butter
1 Cup Sugar
4 Eggs
* Cake Tin

Directions
1. Preheat the Air Fryer to 350 degrees
2. Melt half of the butter with the dark chocolate in a thick-bottomed pan, and melt the white chocolate in another pan with the rest of the butter. Leave to cool
3. Beat the eggs with the sugar and vanilla extract. Divide the flour into two portions and add a pinch of salt to each
4. Beat half of the egg-sugar mixture through the dark chocolate. Then add in half of the flour and half of the nuts and mix. Do the same with the white chocolate mixture
5. Pour the white and brown brownie mixture into two different sides of the cake tin. Use a spatula to partially mix the two colors, creating a swirl
6. Place tray into the Air Fryer and bake the brownies for 30 minutes. When ready, the surface should be dry to touch

CHOCOLATE CAKE

Ingredients
1/4 Cup Sugar
2 Ozs Butter
1 Egg
1 Tbsp Apricot Jam
2 Ozs Flour
1 Tbsp Cocoa
Cooking Spray
Salt to taste
1 Tsp Icing Sugar
* Small Ring Cake Tin

Directions
1. Preheat the Air Fryer to 320 degrees
2. Spray the cake tin with the cooking spray
3. In a bowl, beat the sugar with the softened butter until light and creamy. Add the egg and jam then combine into the butter
4. Sift in the flour, cocoa powder and salt. Mix thoroughly
5. Transfer the batter to the cake tin and use a spatula to level the surface
6. Put the cake tin in the Air Fryer tray. Set the timer for 15 minutes and bake until a knife inserted in the center of the cake comes out cleanly

CHOCOLATE CHERRY POUND CAKE

Ingredients
2/3 Cup Flour
1 Cup Dark Chocolate Chips
1/2 Cup Cocoa Powder, melted
2/3 Cup Unsalted Butter, softened
3 Ozs Icing Sugar
1/2 Tsp Baking Powder
12 Cherries, halved and pithed
Zest and Juice of 1 Lemon
Pinch of Salt
3 Eggs
* Loaf Pan

Directions
1. Preheat the Air Fryer at 320 degrees
2. Cream butter, sugar and lemon zest using an electric mixer until light and fluffy. Beat in eggs one at a time until well mixed
3. Next add in cocoa powder, chocolate chips, sieved flour, baking powder, salt and lemon juice. Combine all ingredients to form a batter
4. Pour batter into the loaf pan. Arrange the cherries on top of the batter
5. Place the loaf pan into the Air Fryer and cook for 25 minutes. Check the cake at around 20 minutes or until a skewer insert in the middle and comes out clean

CHOCOLATE FONDANT

Ingredients
4 Ozs Chocolate
1 Cup Self Raising Flour
3 Ozs Brown Sugar
1 Oz Butter
1/4 Cup Milk
Cooking Spray
1 Egg
* 4 Small Ramekins

Directions
1. In a pan over low heat, melt the chocolate until it has a liquid consistency. Slowly stir in the milk and butter
2. Whisk the sugar and egg together in a bowl. Continue mixing until it forms a creamy texture, then pour the contents into the chocolate mixture. Slowly stir in the flour, ensuring that there are no lumps
3. Grease the ramekins a coating of cooking spray. Fill each one with the batter mixture
4. Heat the Air Fryer to 350 degrees
5. Arrange the ramekins in the Air Fryer and bake for 4 minutes or more until the fondant is crispy on top
6. Serve with vanilla ice cream

CINNAMON CRISPAS

Ingredients
Flour Tortillas
1/2 Tsp Cinnamon
2/3 Cup Icing Sugar
Honey to serve

Directions
1. Preheat the Air Fryer to 350 degrees
2. Cut flour tortillas into quarters
3. Place tortilla pieces into the Air Fryer tray and cook for 2 to 3 minutes until crisp
4. Combine sugar and cinnamon into a bag. Toss fried tortillas into the sugar mixture and shake until coated
5. Spread with honey to serve for additional flavor

CINNAMON DOUGHNUTS

Ingredients
For the Doughnuts:
2 Tbsps Butter
1/2 Cup Sugar
3 Cups Self Raising Flour
2 Egg Yolks
1/2 Cup Sour Cream
1/4 Cup Butter, melted

For the Cinnamon Sugar:
1/3 Cup Sugar
1 Tsp Cinnamon

Directions
1. Slowly combine the flour and sour cream together and knead to form a dough. Add some milk if required to achieved a firmer texture
2. On a clean floured surface, roll the dough so that it is 1cm in thickness. Use the head of a cup to cut out circular shapes, then use the head of the shot glass to remove a circle from the center
3. Heat the Air Fryer to 375 degrees
4. Combine the egg yolks, butter and sugar in a bowl. Taking a brush, cover each side of the doughnuts with the mixture
5. Place the doughnuts into the Air Fryer and cook for 7 or more minutes. Remove when the doughnut is firm and lightly browned, then brush again with the butter mix and sprinkle with cinnamon sugar to serve

COCONUT FLAN

Ingredients
3/4 Cup Canned Coconut Milk
1/4 Cup Evaporated Milk
1/4 Cup Sweetened Condensed Milk
1/4 Cup Toasted Coconut Flakes
1/2 Cup Sugar
Cooking Spray
2 Eggs and 1 Egg Yolk
* 3 Ramekins

Directions
1. Lightly coat the ramekins with cooking spray
2. Preheat the Air Fryer to 320 degrees
3. In a small pot, add the sugar and 1 ½ tablespoons of water together. Cook over medium-high heat, swirling the pan constantly, until the sugar turns a rich amber color, about 10 minutes
4. Immediately pour 1 tablespoon of the caramel into the bottom of each ramekin
5. In a mixing bowl, blend the 3 milks with a whisk adding the eggs and egg yolk last
6. Once well blended, ladle the custard base into the ramekins. Cover each ramekin with aluminum foil and bake for 30 minutes in the Air Fryer
7. Remove the ramekins and uncover, place into the refrigerator for 2 hours to set completely
8. Once set, add the coconut flakes on top of the flan and serve with orange sauce

CRUNCHY SNICKERS

Ingredients
4 Snickers Bars
2/3 Cup Flour
1 Tsp Baking Powder
1 Egg, beaten
1/2 Cup Water
Chocolate Sauce
Icing Sugar
Whipped Cream

Directions
1. Preheat the Air Fryer to 350 degrees
2. Combine the flour and baking powder in a bowl and form a well in the center and add the egg. Gradually add the water, whisking, until you have a smooth batter
3. Coat the Snickers bars in the batter, shaking off excess. Fry the bars in the Air Fryer tray for 1 to 2 minutes or until golden
4. Drizzle with chocolate sauce, sprinkle with icing sugar and serve with cream

FRIED BANANAS

Ingredients
2 Bananas
1 Tbsp Butter, melted
1 Tbsp Brown Sugar
1 Cup Panko Breadcrumbs

Directions
1. Preheat the Air Fryer to 350 degrees
2. In a bowl, mix the brown sugar and breadcrumbs together
3. Slice the bananas into one inch thick chunks and add to the bowl mixture to coat
4. Place bananas in the Air Fryer tray and cook for 10 minutes
5. Serve warm with hot fudge sauce and ice cream, if desired

FRIED CHOC CHIP COOKIE DOUGH

Ingredients
For the Dough:
2 ½ Cups Plain Flour
1 Tsp Vanilla Extract
2 Cups Chocolate Chips
1 Tsp Baking Soda
1 Tsp Salt
1 Cup Butter
2 Cups Sugar
2 Eggs

For the Batter:
2 Cups Plain Flour
2 Tbsps Sugar
1 Tsp Baking Powder
1/2 Cup Club Soda
1 Egg

Directions
1. To form the dough, combine the flour, baking soda, and salt. In another bowl, beat the butter using a mixer then gradually add the vanilla extract and sugar until it forms soft peaks. Slowly add the flour mixture until it forms a dough. Finish by adding the chocolate chips
2. Take spoonfuls of the dough and roll into even sized balls. Set aside in the freezer for 20 minutes to firm
3. To make the batter, combine the egg, club soda, baking powder, flour and sugar
4. Preheat the Air Fryer to 390 degrees
5. When the dough balls are ready, dip into the batter mixture to coat. Place them the Air Fryer tray and cook for 6 minutes until crispy
6. Best served warm

FRIED MADERIA ICE CREAM BITES

Ingredients
2/3 Cup Madeira Cake, crumbled
4 Scoops Vanilla Ice Cream
Caramel Topping

Directions
1. Place the cake crumbs into the Air Fryer at 350 degrees for 5 minutes or until golden brown and crisp. Shake the crumbs occasionally for even crispness
2. Transfer to a plate and set aside for 5 minutes to cool
3. Taking one scoop at a time, roll the ice cream in the crumb mixture and coat evenly
4. Place ice cream bites into serving bowls and drizzle with caramel topping

FRIED MARS BARS

Ingredients
1 Mars Bar
1 Cup Flour
1/2 Cup Cornflour
1 Pinch Baking Soda
1 Cup Milk

Directions
1. Chill the chocolate bar by keeping it in the fridge, but do not freeze it
2. Mix the flour, cornflour and baking soda together. Add milk to the mixture until you get a batter with the consistency of thin cream
3. Preheat the Air Fryer to 350 degrees
4. Remove wrapper from the chilled chocolate bar and coat completely in batter
5. Place the coated bar into the Air Fryer tray and cook for 5 minutes or until crispy
6. Serve with ice cream

FRIED OREOS

Ingredients
1 Bag Oreos
2 Cups Pancake Mix
1 ½ Cups Milk
2 Eggs
3 Tsps Oil

Directions
1. Heat the Air Fryer to 350 degrees
1. In a bowl, combine the milk, pancake mix, eggs and oil. Ensure there are no lumps
2. Open the Oreos and place each biscuit into the batter mixture. The cookies should be completely covered
3. Place battered Oreos into the Air Fryer tray and cook for 3 minutes until crispy
4. Serve whilst hot

FRIED STRAWBERRIES

Ingredients
24 Strawberries
1 Cup Pancake Mix
2/3 Cup Milk
Icing Sugar

Directions
1. Preheat the Air Fryer to 350 degrees
2. Combine the pancake mix with the milk and stir well until it forms a thick batter
3. Dip the strawberries in the batter and place in the Air Fryer tray. Cook for 7 minutes until crispy
4. Place fried strawberries onto a platter and cover lightly with icing sugar

FRUIT CAKE

Ingredients
1/2 Cup Dried Fruits
1/2 Cup All Purpose Flour
1/2 Cup Icing Sugar
1/2 Cup Butter
1/2 Tsp Vanilla Extract
Pinch of Ginger Powder
Pinch of Cinnamon Powder
1/2 Tsp Baking Powder
2 Eggs
* Round Cake Tin

Directions
1. Preheat the Air Fryer at 350 degrees
2. In a bowl, mix in the butter and cream with a blender. Once the butter is softened, slowly add the sugar, vanilla and egg and blend until light and fluffy
3. In a separate bowl, add the flour, dried fruits, ginger powder, cinnamon powder and baking powder and mix well
4. Sift the flour mixture in the butter mixture and fold together. Spoon the mixture into the greased cake tin
5. Place the cake tin in the Air Fryer and bake for about 16 minutes
6. Allow to cool and sprinkle with icing sugar to serve

FRUIT MUFFINS

Ingredients
1 Pack Oreo Biscuits
1 Tsp Lemon Juice
2 Cups Chopped Fruits
1/2 Tsp Baking powder
1/4 Tsp Cooking Soda
1/4 Tsp Ground Cinnamon
1 Tsp Honey
1 Cup Milk
* 4 Silicon Muffin Cups

Directions
1. Crush the biscuits in a bowl and add milk to form a smooth batter. Add baking powder, cooking soda, and cocoa power then mix well
2. Pour the batter into the muffin cups and place into the preheated Air Fryer for 10 minutes at 320 degrees
3. In a bowl, mix all chopped fruits, honey, cinnamon powder and lemon juice together
4. Once the muffins are ready, allow to cool until lukewarm. Scoop the center portion of each muffin out and replace with the chopped fruit mixture
5. Muffins can be stored in refrigerator or at room temperature

GLAZED HONEY PEARS

Ingredients
4 Pears, halved
Pinch of Saffron
1/4 Cup Honey
1 Cup Greek Yoghurt

Directions
1. Preheat the Air Fryer to 350 degrees
2. Place the pear halves into the Air Fryer tray and cook for 6 minutes. They should be brown, soft and slightly caramelized
3. In a separate bowl, combine the honey, yoghurt and saffron
4. Open the Air Fryer tray and pour the mixture over the pears. Resume cooking for another 5 minutes
5. Serve with a side of cream or sprinkled with cinnamon or nuts

LEMON CREAM CHEESE BARS

Ingredients
2 Cans Crescent Roll Dough
Juice and Zest of 2 Lemons
2 Cups Cream Cheese
1 Cup Sugar
2 Tbsps Butter, melted
* Baking Dish

Directions
1. Preheat the Air Fryer to 350 degrees
2. Place a can of the dough along the base of the baking dish, ensuring that all edges are covered
3. In a bowl, add all of the lemon juice and zest from 1 ½ of the lemons, cream cheese and half of the sugar. Use a mixer to combine until it forms a creamy texture. Pour the mixture over the base of the layered baking dish
4. Taking the other can of dough, unroll and place over the cream cheese layer. Stretch the dough towards the edges of the baking dish. Cover the dough with the melted butter, brushing so it is well coated
5. Combine the remaining zest and sugar together. Sprinkle over the buttered top layer of dough
6. Place tray into the Air Fryer and bake for 30 minutes.
7. When the cream cheese bars have cooled, invert the baking dish and remove the dessert. Place into the refrigerator for an hour to firm and then slice into bars

LEMON MERINGUE SPONGE

Ingredients

For the Meringue:
1 Cup Self Raising Flour
1 Cup Sugar
1 Cup Butter
3 Eggs
1/4 Tsp Baking Powder
1 Tbsp Grated Lemon Zest
1 Tsp Vanilla Extract
Cooking Spray

For the Frosting:
3/4 Cup Sugar
4 Egg Whites

* Baking Tin

Directions
1. Preheat the Air Fryer to 320 degrees
2. Prepare the baking tin by coating with cooking spray
3. Place all the meringue ingredients into a mixer and combine at high speed until the creamy and thick
4. Spoon the batter into the baking tin (may require two batches). Place in the Air Fryer and bake for 15 minutes. The cake should be soft to the touch and a light sand color
5. Whilst the cake is cooking, start to prepare the frosting. You will need a beater, metal mixing bowl and a pot with simmering water
6. Poor the egg whites and sugar into the metal bowl and place over the simmering water. Ensure that the bowl does not touch the water. Beat the egg whites and sugar until fluffy and it forms soft peaks
7. Spread generously over the cooled cake and top with preferred garnish

LEMON MUFFINS

Ingredients
2 Tsps Lemon Juice
1/2 Cup Self Raising Flour
1/2 Tsp Baking Powder
1/2 Cup Butter
4 Ozs Cream Cheese
1/2 Cup Sugar
Pinch of Salt
1/2 Cup Raspberries
2 Eggs
* Silicon Muffin Cups

Directions
1. Allow the butter and cream cheese to warm to room temperature before mixing. Once softened, slice the slab of butter and cream cheese into smaller cubes. Beat the cubes until it has a creamy consistency
2. Add the sugar and beat until the mixture is light and fluffy
3. Beat in the eggs, adding them one at a time
4. Fold in the flour and salt, then add the lemon juice
5. Once the mixture is ready, spoon it into silicon cups and top each one with some raspberries
6. Place cups into the Air Fryer at 365 degrees for 20 minutes. Poke the cupcakes with a toothpick to check if they are cooked through

MARBLE CAKE

Ingredients
2/3 Cup Butter, melted
1/2 Cup Sugar
2 Tsps Cocoa Powder
1/2 Cup Self Raising Flour, sieved
1/2 Tsp Lemon Juice
Cooking Spray
3 Eggs
* Round Cake Pan

Directions
1. Preheat the Air Fryer at 350 degrees
2. Grease and line the cake pan with the cooking spray
3. Add 1/3 of the melted butter into a bowl and mix in the cocoa powder. Combine until it forms a smooth paste
4. Beat the remaining melted butter with the lemon juice and sugar until it is pale. Beat the eggs, and add into the butter mixture, alternating with the flour until smooth
5. Pour the cake batter into the greased cake pan, alternating the cocoa mixture. Use a knife or skewer to create a swirl pattern
6. Bake for 15 to 17 minutes in the Air Fryer
7. Allow the marble cake to cool before serving

MATCHA ALMOND COOKIES

Ingredients
2 Tsps Matcha Powder
2 Tbsps Almonds, chopped
2 Tbsps Butter
2 Tbsps Icing Sugar
1/4 Cup All Purpose Flour
Pinch of Salt

Directions
1. Using an mixer, cream the butter and sugar until light and fluffy
2. In another bowl, sift the flour, matcha powder and salt together
3. Using a spatula, mix the ingredients in the two bowls and the chopped almonds together to form a dough
4. Roll the dough into a ball and wrap tightly in cling film. Allow to cool in the refrigerator for half an hour
5. Preheat the Air Fryer at 320 degrees
6. Roll dough into small balls and arrange them on the Air Fryer tray. Use a knife to flatten each ball
7. Bake the cookies for 13 minutes until desired consistency is achieved

MINI APPLE PIES

Ingredients
3 Apples, chopped
1 Tbsp Lemon Juice
2 Tsps Flour
2 Tsps Cinnamon
2 Tsps Brown Sugar
1/2 Tsp Nutmeg
1/2 Tsp Ground Cloves
10 Sheets of Filo Pastry, thawed
3/4 Cup Butter, melted

Directions
1. In a bowl, mix together the apples, lemon juice, flour, sugar and spices to form the filling
2. Place the filo pastry onto a clean counter and gently brush with butter
3. Place a third cup of apple pie filling in the middle of the filo sheet, about two inches from the bottom of the sheet
4. Continue to fold the filling up until a triangle is formed. Brush the entire triangle with butter
5. Sprinkle with sugar, if desired
6. Cook two or three at a time in the Air Fryer at 320 degrees for 6 to 8 minutes
7. Cook until lightly brown and apples are soft when pierced with a toothpick. Allow to cool slightly before serving
8. Serve with whipped cream or ice cream

PANDAN CHIFFON CAKE

Ingredients
3 Egg Yolks
1 Tbsp Sugar
1/2 Cup Cake Flour
1/2 Tsp Baking Powder
1/4 Cup Coconut Milk
1 Tsp Concentrated Pandan Juice

For the Egg White:
3 Egg Whites
2 ½ Tbsps Sugar
1/4 Tsp Cream Of Tartar

For the Pandan Juice:
10 Pandan Leaves
2 Tbsps Water

* Cake Tin

Directions
1. To extract the pandan juice, cut the pandan leaves into chunks and place into a food processor with the water. Process into small pieces. Place mixture in a muslin bag and squeeze out the juice. Refrigerate for 15 minutes to allow the juice to set
2. In a separate bowl, beat egg yolks with the sugar until light and creamy. Add coconut milk and pandan juice into the mixture and combine well
3. In another bowl, beat the egg white until foamy and add the cream of tartar whilst mixing
4. Slowly add sugar into the bowl. Continue to beat the egg white mixture till stiff peaks form
5. Spoon 1/3 egg white and fold into the egg yolk mixture till well mixed. Lightly fold in the rest of the egg whites with spatula until combined
6. Preheat the Air Fryer at 320 degrees

7. Line the bottom of the cake tin, then pour in the batter. Ensure that there is room for the cake to rise by only filling three quarters of the tin
8. Put the cake tin into the Air Fryer and bake for approximately 30 minutes
9. Once cake is baked, do a skewer test check to ensure the batter is fully cooked
10. Remove cake tin from the Air Fryer, invert, and allow the cake to cool completely before unmolding

PEANUT COOKIES

Ingredients
1 Cup Peanut Butter
2 Cups All Purpose Flour
2/3 Cup Vegetable Oil
1/2 Cup Icing Sugar
Pinch of Salt
1 Egg Yolk, beaten

Directions:
1. Place all the ingredients in mixing bowl and mix evenly with hand until a soft dough is formed. Chill in the fridge for about 30 minutes, covered in cling film
2. Preheat the Air Fryer at 340 degrees
3. Roll dough into small flattened balls about 2-3 cm in diameter and arrange them onto the Air Fryer tray
4. Using the egg yolk, glaze the surface with egg yolk and bake for about 10 to 12 minutes or until the top is golden brown

RED VELVET CUPCAKES

Ingredients
For the Batter:
3/4 Cup Icing Sugar
3/4 Cup Peanut butter
1 Tsp Cocoa Powder
2 Tsps Beet Powder
2 Cups Flour
3 Eggs

For the Icing:
3/4 Cup Icing Sugar
1 Cup Butter
1 Tsp Vanilla Essence
1 Cup Cream Cheese

* Silicon Cupcake Molds

Directions
1. To prepare the batter, add all ingredients in a bowl. Beat well with a whisk
2. Fill each cupcake mold with the batter mixture
3. Preheat the Air Fryer at 350 degrees
4. Insert the molds into the Air Fryer tray and cook the cupcakes for 10 to 12 minutes. Set aside until cool
5. To prepare the frosting, add all ingredients into a bowl and beat until it has a smooth and thick consistency
6. Top the cooled cupcakes with the frosting and other preferred garnish

SPICY PINEAPPLE FRITTERS

Ingredients
2 Cups Pineapple, chopped
1 Habanero Chili, minced
Salt and Pepper to taste
1 Tbsp Fresh Chives, diced
1 Scallion, diced
1/2 Tsp Turmeric
3 Sage Leaves, minced
1 Cup Flour
1/2 Cup Milk
2 Eggs

Directions
1. Preheat the Air Fryer to 350 degrees
2. Combine all ingredients except the pineapple in a blender until smooth and well mixed
3. Place in a bowl and add pineapple chunks. Stir to coat
4. Place the battered pineapple fritters into the Air Fryer tray and fry till browned for 2 to 3 minutes
5. Season with salt before serving

SUGARED BEIGNETS

Ingredients
1/4 Cup Sugar
1 ¼ Ozs Dry Yeast
1 Egg
1/4 Cup Buttermilk, warmed
1/4 Cup Milk, warmed
1 Tsp Salt
1/2 Tsp Baking Soda
4 Cups Bread Flour
1/4 Cup Unsalted Butter
Icing Sugar

Directions
1. In a large bowl, combine the yeast, sugar and 3/4 cup of warm water. Allow to rest until it becomes foamy. Add the salt, egg, buttermilk, milk, baking soda, and bread flour and mix until it forms a dough. Melt the butter and slowly add until the dough is no longer tacky
2. Knead the dough until it has a smooth texture with no lumps. Allow to rest in a covered bowl for an hour
3. On a clean, floured surface, roll the rested dough until it is a half inch thick. Cut 2 inch squares out and place onto a baking sheet. Enclose with cling wrap and leave for half an hour so that the pastry has puffed
4. Heat the Air Fryer to 390 degrees
5. Place beignets in the Air Fryer tray for 3 to 4 minutes until crispy
6. Sprinkle with icing sugar to serve

TWICE BAKED NUT COOKIES

Ingredients
4 Cups Flour
4 Eggs
1 Tsp Baking Powder
1 Cup Oil
1 Cup Chopped Nuts
1/2 Tsp Salt
1 Tsp Vanilla Essence
1 Cup Sugar

Directions
1. Beat together eggs, oil, sugar and vanilla. Sift flour with salt and baking powder. Add to other ingredients and mix well. Stir in nuts, mixing well. Refrigerate for several hours or overnight
2. Shape mixture into rolls that will fit in the Air Fryer tray
3. Preheat the Air Fryer to 375 degrees
4. Bake for about 35 minutes or until golden. Slice into 1/2 inch thick slices while still warm
5. Place each slice on its side and sprinkle with a mixture of cinnamon and sugar
6. Return to the Air Fryer and bake for about 10 more minutes to dry

VANILLA SOUFFLE

Ingredients
1/4 Cup Flour
1/4 Cup Butter, melted
1 Cup Milk
1/4 Cup Sugar
2 Tsps Vanilla Extract
1 Vanilla Bean
5 Egg Whites and 4 Egg Yolks
1 Tsp Cream of Tartar
Cooking Spray
Icing Sugar
* 6 Small Ramekin Cups

Directions
1. Combine the melted butter and flour in a bowl until there are no lumps
2. In a pan, dissolve the sugar into the milk. Then add the vanilla bean and allow to boil. Pour the butter mixture into the boiling milk. Reduce to a simmer until the components thicken, then remove the pan from the heat and cool mixture using an ice bath. Discard the vanilla bean
3. Once cooled, mix in the vanilla extract and egg yolks. Combine well
4. Prepare each ramekin by greasing lightly with the cooking spray
5. Whisk the sugar, cream of tartar and egg whites in a bowl until fluffy peaks form. Combine with the milk soufflé base and carefully place the mixture into the ramekins
6. Preheat the Air Fryer to 340 degrees
7. Place half of the soufflé cups into the cooking tray and cook each batch for 12 or more minutes
8. Serve garnished with icing sugar

ABOUT THE AUTHOR

JUSTIN RAMSEY

Growing up in the food industry, Justin's family operated a range of traditional and western inspired restaurants. His passion for hearty and wholesome meals enabled him to build his own catering business.

He lives in Portland, Oregon with his wife and twin girls. Justin loves educating and inspiring other families to cook and move away from processed ingredients.

Stay connected to Justin's future publications at
www.bookwormhaven.com

One Last Thing...

If you enjoyed this book or found it useful I'd be very grateful if you'd post a short review on Amazon.

Your support really does make a difference and I read all the reviews personally so I can get your feedback and make this book even better.

Thanks again for your support!

Justin